WE CAN WORK IT OUT

WE CAN WORK IT OUT

Creative

Conflict Resolution

with

Your TEEN

Rodney Gage

Broadman & Holman Publishers

Nashville, Tennessee

© 2002 by Rodney Gage
All rights reserved

Printed in the United States of America

0-8054-2422-9

Published by Broadman & Holman Publishers,
Nashville, Tennessee

Subject Heading: PARENTING

Unless otherwise stated all Scripture citation is from the NIV, the Holy Bible, New International Version, copyright © 1973, 1978, 1984 by International Bible Society; Other versions cited are NASB, the New American Standard Bible, © the Lockman Foundation, 1960, 1962, 1963, 1968, 1971, 1972, 1973, 1975, 1977; used by permission; New King James Version, copyright © 1979, 1980, 1982, Thomas Nelson, Inc., Publishers; RSV, Revised Standard Version of the Bible, copyrighted 1946, 1952, © 1971, 1973; and the King James Version.

1 2 3 4 5 6 7 8 9 10   06 05 04 03 02

DEDICATION

This book is dedicated to my wonderful wife Michelle and our three children Rebecca, Ashlyn, and Luke. Through God's love and grace, I commit to modeling the message of this book in my life. I love each of you very deeply.

TABLE OF CONTENTS

	How to Use This Book	viii
1.	Perspective Makes All the Difference	1
2.	Don't Fence Me In!	11
3.	Is History Repeating Itself?	26
4.	How Much Is Too Much?	46
5.	The Truth and Nothing but the Truth	67
6.	Get a H.A.N.D.L.E. on Resolving Conflict	80
7.	Constructive Consequences	93
8.	Managing Anger	111
9.	A Reduced-Stress Environment	126
10.	Forgiveness . . . and Other Longings	138
11.	Creating an Atmosphere of Peace	153
12.	Living in Hope	170
	Endnotes	182
	About the Author	184

HOW TO USE THIS BOOK

Over the years, I have counseled with hundreds of parents one-on-one who feel overwhelmed and defeated due to the relational challenges they're facing with their teens. The fact that you have picked up the book is a wonderful accomplishment in itself because it would be very easy for you just to throw in the towel and quit. Most parents who struggle with frequent conflict with their teen often feel as if they are the only ones experiencing problems in their home. You may be surprised to find the number of parents who can identify with the same challenges you're facing. This is the reason why parents need the encouragement and support that comes from a small group. Experts agree that one of the strongest methods to enrich relationships happens in small groups.

Apart from the individual time you invest reading through this book, I highly recommend working through it with other parents as well. Learning from one another's experiences and sharing your prayer requests and praise reports with other parents is a great way to find encouragement.

I encourage you to share this book with your youth pastor or pastor and ask if you can start a small group specifically for parents of teens. If you feel unqualified or lack the confidence to pull a group of parents together, find someone to help you. You could begin meeting in someone's home or a local coffee shop. Each member of the group can read one or two chapters a week and work through the questions at the end of each chapter. These questions are designed to help parents reflect on the different areas in their relationships that will help them grow spiritually, emotionally, and relationally.

I pray this book and the companion resources listed in the back of this book will contain the answers and hope you're looking for to bring healing and health to your family. I believe the ministry we have to our family is the most important ministry we will ever have. I pray for God's richest blessings upon you and your teen.

Hang in there; the best is yet to come!

Rodney Gage, Jeremiah 29:11

ONE

PERSPECTIVE MAKES ALL THE DIFFERENCE

I talk with parents every week—parents who sincerely love their teenagers and want only what's best for them. As I listen to these parents, I notice one problem they struggle with more than any other: *conflict*. Many of them tell me that constant conflict with their teenager makes their family relationships look like the first-down markers at a football game—they're chained together but always ten yards apart.

Ask the Right Question

Perspective makes all the difference. How we look at conflict determines how we handle it, and that perspective colors our reactions, responses, and, ultimately, the quality of that precious relationship with our teenagers. Many parents have one supreme goal: to end the argument as soon as possible. They can't stand the fussing and fighting or the rolling eyes and the withdrawal, so they use strategies to eliminate the tension as soon as they possibly can. Perhaps the most important thing you will get out of this book is this: that goal is wrong. Trying to control a teenager's behavior ultimately will increase tension, create more conflict, and drive a deeper wedge between parents and teenagers (and often, between the parents themselves). A better goal is to use the conflict creatively to learn and grow, both you and your teenager, and yes, your spouse too. The question is not, How can I end the tension as quickly as possible? but rather, How can this tension propel us to understand one another more deeply and build trust more soundly than ever before?

Instead of running from the conflict or blasting the person to control him, this goal calls for a different strategy—emotional control, talking, listening, honesty, and clear enforceable boundaries. Our behavior changes from controlling others to giving them choices. Then we honor those choices with positive or negative consequences. In this way we treat our teens more like adults . . . and we act more like adults. When we act and treat them this way, we move a long way down the road toward helping them become independent, mature, responsible adults. And ultimately, that's a primary purpose of parenting.

Many parents and teenagers experience tension over the commonplace issues of adolescence: grades, being home on time, friends, and money. Today, new topics are on that list of conflict producers: the challenge of our children considering interracial dating, too much time on the Internet, and online pornography. Some young people experience significant problems: drugs, guns, vandalism, stealing, and cheating. All of these difficulties are intensified by the pain of broken families, and they are made far more complex and confusing when broken families become blended families.

Melissa's Story

One night after I spoke to a group of parents, a mother named Nancy approached me to share the remarkable story of her daughter

Melissa. I was so moved, I asked if she would be willing to put it in writing to give hope and encouragement to those reading this book. She wrote:

> Dear Rodney,
>
> When Melissa started dating Cory, we were very concerned because we felt he was a very deceptive person. You could just feel it by being around him. He was smooth and manipulative, and we were afraid Melissa didn't see it—and she didn't.
>
> But the more we expressed our concern, the more determined she was to be involved with him. We saw evidence of a physical relationship: touching, hands on each other, a little too friendly! And it turned out, it was more than we thought it was.
>
> We saw problems in their relationship, but it seemed that everything we did to try to fix it was exactly the wrong thing. If we tried to be firm, that made it a lot worse. We'd always been a pretty strict family with high standards, and I guess our rules were pretty rigid. We tried to bend—even more than we thought we should—but we desperately were trying to do what was best for Melissa. We thought that if they got too involved, if she got pregnant, if they got married, it would be a disaster! It would never work out. But no matter what we tried to do, she became angry and more determined to do it her way.
>
> We felt like we were trapped in a terrible situation. No matter what we did, it wasn't right. We saw Melissa sliding down a very dangerous path. In fact, I was afraid she was going to run away from home. She got so angry, especially with her dad. They got in yelling matches, and she told him, "I hate you! I want to get

out of here!" One night, I felt it was imminent. I told her, "Melissa, I want you to go to the youth event at church tonight, but when it's over, I want you to meet us downstairs so we can go home right away."

I felt bad because I needed to go check on her. In fact, I wanted to go sit with her, but Stewart said, "No, let's don't do that. She needs to feel that we trust her." So I let her go on her own. I felt strongly that something was wrong. A little while later, I went to check on her, but she was gone. Somebody said she had been seen with Cory. That began a night that forever changed our lives. My life will never be the same. . . .

Consider This . . .

I will share the rest of Nancy's story later in this book, but first let me ask you a few questions:

- Have you ever been hurt or disappointed by your son's or daughter's attitudes or actions?
- Do you feel like you're in a losing battle with your teenager?
- Instead of working together to find win-win solutions that benefit both of you, do you feel like your teenager seemingly finds a way to get what he or she wants?
- Does the feeling of having a lack of control over your teen make you feel angry?
- Does the feeling of losing control make you want to strike back to prove who's really in charge?

Unfortunately, when conflict happens in relationships—especially between parents and teenagers—many families feel trapped in a lose-lose situation. Instead of using conflict to strengthen their relationships and draw them closer together, they allow conflict to separate and isolate. Each person feels angry; resentment grows; and everybody loses.

As I have listened to countless stories from parents and teens over the years, I have learned that conflict between a parent and a teenager is a magnifying glass that exposes the true nature of their relationship. As you've learned from Nancy's story, when a relationship is shallow or underdeveloped, conflict results in hardened hearts and hostility toward each other. In contrast, when a deep relationship has been pursued and cultivated, conflict can result in mutual growth and understanding.

The Classroom

I don't believe it's a coincidence that you picked up this book. I believe God has a purpose for everything. God wants to use this book as a lifeline to help you face the challenges of raising your teenager. The conflict or circumstances you're facing with your teenager might not be on the level my friend Nancy faced with her daughter, but the stress you experience from the day-to-day battles may be draining you emotionally, relationally, and spiritually. Perhaps you sense that things are already headed in a downward spiral, and you want to get control of the situation before it's too late.

Allow conflict to be a classroom to teach you and your teenager important lessons. If you see it that way, you can embrace the tension as a gift. Too much conflict, however, can shatter the individuals involved as well as the relationship. This book is designed to help you lower the tension level so that the discussions become productive, not destructive.

Whether we like it or not, conflict is inevitable. Show me a relationship that has any time and experience to it, and I'll show you conflict. The disputes may explode or they may be as quiet as a smoldering fire, but some form of strife inevitably happens between any two people who relate to each other, especially between parents and teenagers. The real tragedy, though, is that most parents have no idea how to handle the everyday conflicts that cause misunderstanding and hurt in their relationships with their teenagers. If that hurt is not resolved, it will turn into something more sinister and damaging. While it is still hurt, we need to be honest about it. In his book *Do-It-Yourself Relationship Mender,* Dr. Gary Rosberg wrote: "Offenses come in all shapes and sizes, but they all wound. Just as physical trauma penetrates our human skin, so relational offenses penetrate our emotional skin. In fact, the impact can be like sending a cannonball through the heart of an unsuspecting bystander.... The offense is usually a distinct event. If it's dealt with immediately, it may not have any lasting consequences. But in most cases, the person who was offended has time to think about it and stew over it. What develops is the emotion of hurt. Not anger or rage. Not bitterness and resentment. Those come later if the hurt is not dealt with. Hurt acts as a barometer measuring our response to the threats of our world. Hurt is the emotion of vulnerability."[1]

Be Realistic

If you are struggling with conflict with your teenager—*relax!* You're not a bad person, and neither is your teenager. Don't beat yourself up with guilt as though you're failing as a parent. In his book *Parenting Adolescents,* author Kevin Huggins observed that being the parent of an adolescent often has devastating effects on us. The arguments and conflict lead us to question our competency to make good decisions, our sanity, and our purpose in life. It shakes the very core of our identity and makes us wonder who we really are. If you feel that way, you can be sure that you aren't alone.

Many of the tensions we experience with teenagers are rooted in fear—the fear of losing control, the fear of the other person walking away, the fear of our spouse turning against us, the fear of others thinking we are incompetent. The more we fear, the more we feel compelled to control those around us. But controlling isn't love, trust, or respect. It communicates that we don't trust the other person, and it leaves us feeling rotten about ourselves—even when we are successful in our controlling attempts!

The tug-of-war in relating to a teenager is, to some degree at least, entirely normal. The hardest thing about the parent-teen relationship is that both parties want to be in control. The parent has to change from being protective when the offspring was a dependent child to gradually trusting the young person to make her own decisions and take responsibility. And the teenager, as we'll see in the next chapter, is going through cataclysmic biological and sociological changes. She demands to be treated like an adult, even if her behavior and attitudes haven't yet earned that trust and freedom. Both parents and teenagers are going through a time of change. If we realize this and address it, we will sail these rough waters with more of a sense of adventure than a sense of dread. For some of us, however, the ship has already hit the shoals and sunk. We need a rescue party and a salvage boat to keep us alive and help us get going again.

No matter how bleak things look right now, no matter how much you fear you are losing the battle, there's hope. God is a fountain of wisdom, and he will guide you. He will give you the strength to make the hard choices you need to make. The process of change may be difficult, but if you keep your mind and heart on the goal of honoring God and producing a young person who becomes a responsible, independent adult, you can make it.

Learning the Hard Way

The principles in this book are not just academic to me. When I was a teenager, I experienced gut-wrenching conflict in our family.

My goal for writing this book is very personal. God has taken me through the process of learning, growing, and healing, and I believe he wants to do that in countless other individual lives and families. My goal is to help you discover how you can actually use conflict, in a creative way, to be a doorway to meaningful communication with your teenager.

Rodney's Story

I grew up as a preacher's kid. My father was a nationally known itinerate evangelist. Therefore, he was away from home a lot while we were growing up. My father and mother both came from highly dysfunctional families. The only way they knew how to handle their emotions and communicate with each other, and with us as children, was to reflect what they saw modeled in their own homes growing up. Even though my parents became Christians after they were married and my father entered the ministry, there was still a lot of emotional baggage the two of them never learned to deal with. Like many families, anger, manipulation, threats, and withdrawal became the norm even in our home. Please don't misunderstand me, I have two wonderful parents who, in fact, provided a strong spiritual upbringing that I'll talk about in the last chapter.

However, our family never learned how to talk through problems. We had rules and expectations, and if the rules and expectations were not met, there was punishment—or at least threats of punishment. I always wanted, but never got, the opportunity to tell Dad our side of the story. We never felt the freedom to approach him with an opinion or a reason or an excuse. Our mother protected us. When she saw my dad handling things by using anger or threats, or when she saw the punishment didn't fit the crime, she tried to step in and tell him to ease up. But her attempts to fix things always created conflict between them—blaming and accusations.

Unresolved conflict usually creates more conflict. A dispute between a father and a son affects all the children as well as the relationship between husband and wife. The tension may subside for a few days or until the next conflict comes along. In our family, feelings were seldom expressed so as to reveal the real needs in our lives. Instead, we hid our feelings as much as we could or exploded in anger. Even in a Christian home, this is a common cycle of handling conflict. People allow their emotions to take control instead of taking control of their emotions. In my family today, my wife Michelle and I are trying hard to break this cycle. It takes effort, commitment, and prayer; it also takes a united effort from both of us. We are praying that with God's help, we will break this unhealthy cycle of behavior and build a different legacy for our children.

I want other families, parents, and kids to avoid what I experienced. I want people to learn how to make life more enjoyable so that conflict is not robbing them of joy and happiness.

Looking Ahead

The next few chapters explore the root causes of conflict between parents and teenagers. You will discover why teenagers sometimes act as though they actually enjoy arguing and fighting with their parents. You will also discover why you, as a parent, respond the way you do toward your teenager when conflict occurs. Even though conflict usually intensifies during the adolescent years, there is a difference between normal and unhealthy conflict. Chapter 2 explains the powerful forces at work in teenagers' hearts.

A Closer Look

1. What are some common causes of conflict between other parents you know and their teenagers?

2. Think about the last couple of weeks. What are the issues that have caused tension between you and your teenager? List those here:

_____

_____

On a scale of 0 (not a problem at all) to 10 (volcano!), rate the intensity of these struggles next to each one you listed.

3. Describe how each person (you, your teenager, your spouse, other children, any other applicable adults) acts when you experience conflict.

4. What do you think it means to see conflict as a classroom?

5. What do you hope God does in your life and your teenager's life as a result of applying the principles in this book?

TWO

DON'T FENCE ME IN!

Teenagers often feel like a rope in a tractor pull—they want to go in both directions, but they feel like they're being ripped apart. They still want and need to be connected to their parents, but at the same time they are getting their feet wet in a quest for independence. A teenager's desire to become independent is a natural, normal, and healthy part of growing and maturing into adulthood. Parents need to understand this fact if they want to keep the communication lines open and maintain healthy relationships with their teenagers.

The struggle between dependence and independence is the proving ground for new attitudes and behaviors. It is the time for growing up. Adolescence is the time when childishness should be eclipsed by maturity, and foolishness replaced by wisdom.

Wisdom: The Goal of Growing Up

We aren't too concerned when little children act foolishly. We don't expect them to be wise and mature. As these children grow into adults, however, our expectations change. Childhood silliness and "cute" mistakes are no longer quite so funny. Instead, the young adult is expected to absorb insight from others and learn from mistakes. This process produces clear thinking and good judgment, a sense of balance between risk and caution—the essence of wisdom. Growth in wisdom is one of the windows through which we can observe adolescents becoming responsible adults. The process of casting off foolish ways and acquiring the ways of wisdom is a wonderful thing to watch in those on that path, but watching a young person continue childish, foolish ways is as painful as a knife wound to those who love him.

The Book of Proverbs has a lot to say about foolishness and wisdom. These passages give insight and instruction about gaining God's perspective on life and making good choices. Here are some samples of what a young person is (or should be) learning:

- A wise person is humble, willing to listen to instruction and trust God: "Do not be wise in your own eyes; fear the LORD and shun evil" (Prov. 3:7).
- A wise person responds well to correction: "Do not rebuke a mocker or he will hate you; rebuke a wise man and he will love you" (Prov. 9:8).
- A wise person thinks through decisions carefully: "Every prudent man acts out of knowledge, but a fool exposes his folly" (Prov. 13:16).
- A wise person chooses wise and godly friends who will have a positive influence on him: "He who walks with the wise grows wise, but a companion of fools suffers harm" (Prov. 13:20).
- A wise person guards his words: "Even a fool is thought wise if he keeps silent, and discerning if he holds his tongue" (Prov. 17:28), and "A fool finds no pleasure in understanding but delights in airing his own opinions" (Prov. 18:2).

- A wise person is in control of his emotions and doesn't let his anger explode: "A fool gives full vent to his anger, but a wise man keeps himself under control" (Prov. 29:11).

Several proverbs also address the relationship between parents and their children. For example:

- A wise person responds to his parents' discipline: "A fool spurns his father's discipline, but whoever heeds correction shows prudence" (Prov. 15:5).
- And finally, a child's choices affect parents profoundly: "A wise son brings joy to his father, but a foolish son grief to his mother" (Prov. 10:1).

These and many other passages about the path of wisdom describe "growing up," especially for Christians. As you read these verses, did you roll your eyes and sigh because your teenager is so far from wisdom? Well, your parents probably did the same thing when they thought of you at that age! Wisdom is not a genetically inherited trait, as are blue eyes or curly hair. No, it is acquired. Even in the best of families, wisdom is learned through trial and error, through experimentation, and through watching the consequences of others' choices.

GUILT AND SELFISHNESS

In his book *Love's Unseen Enemy,* Dr. Les Parrott III observed that many people are plagued by pangs of self-doubt and guilt. They beat themselves up for every mistake, thinking that each failure, no matter how small, reveals a tragic and fatal flaw in themselves. His research showed that while a significant percentage of adults feel this way, almost every adolescent he interviewed was consumed with guilt. Young people desperately want to be independent and free, but they are shackled by intense feelings of inferiority. They lack objectivity to know that these feelings will probably pass as they mature, so they interpret their failures as sweeping, cataclysmic, and permanent. In short, they feel they are trapped in a hopeless pattern of failure.

These feelings of guilt and hopelessness cause a young person's vision to narrow to himself. He becomes very self-centered because he feels the need to protect and prove himself. His selfishness may be understandable when seen from this perspective, but it still drives his parents nuts! Young people often

- demand freedom but want to avoid responsibility.
- look for immediate gratification instead of thinking about future goals.
- show contempt instead of gratitude, even for those who try to help them.
- use explosive anger or sulking withdrawal to manipulate others.
- are absolutely certain they know what's right and refuse to listen to others, especially parents.
- blame anybody and everybody else for their failures.
- demand that parents, siblings, and teachers treat them with respect even if they act like jerks.
- expect others to pay dearly for their mistakes, but expect lots of grace for themselves.
- are greatly offended if anyone questions their actions.
- expect others to make allowances for their schedule, their needs, and their desires.

It's not a pretty picture, is it? Some of this behavior (and a little goes a long way!) is normal at this stage of their lives, but an abundance of it is destructive to the teenager and to those around him. It is important for us to understand the powerful dynamics that push and pull at a teenager's heart.

The Task of Adolescence

Experts who study human behavior have observed that adolescence is the most tumultuous—and perhaps the most important—time in a person's life. The decisions made during this stage are rooted in the stability or instability of childhood, and they have implications for every motive and relationship throughout the rest of the person's life. The supreme task of a teenager is to figure out the answer to the question, Who am I? The answer goes far beyond the facts on a driver's license or the face looking back in the mirror. The young person is on a quest for individuality and independence. She is striving to become someone with values, opinions, and abilities of her own; someone known by her own ideas and accomplishments, not just an extension of her parents.

The privileges they enjoyed as children, such as being protected and provided for, gradually and begrudgingly give way to the responsibilities of adulthood in which they have to protect themselves (and their own families) and make a living. They feel caught between the safety of the past and the risks of the future. Young people yearn to be free, to make their own decisions and take their own risks. Their attitude is "Don't fence me in!" Such an attitude is entirely healthy and appropriate if it is based on a foundation of trust and competency. If young people have this solid foundation, they see the future as a wonderful adventure, but without this foundation, the future is a dark cloud, forboding and ominous.

What does this foundation look like? Some of the crucial elements are:

Trust. Does the young person have a basic sense that those close to her are loving, supportive, and safe? If she does, she will feel connected to her family, and this connection will provide a solid and safe foundation for asking plenty of hard questions. If she doesn't enjoy the stability of trusting relationships, she will feel the need to control people by manipulating them to get the attention she needs.

Independence. Children who develop a basic confidence in their abilities have a far easier time in the storms of adolescence than those who constantly question their ability to perform well. Teenagers experiment with all kinds of new thoughts and new behaviors. If they feel competent and in control, they are more likely to make good decisions and excel in their tasks.

Creativity. Children need to be encouraged to try all kinds of new things, within limits of reason and safety. As they become adolescents, this creativity with limits enables them to see life as an adventure but with dangers they need to avoid. This creativity allows adolescents to become independent without being defiant.

Expertise. As children grow, we see in each the light of particular gifts and abilities. One may be talented musically; another is gifted at math. One may be a terrific athlete; another may have an uncanny ability to lead and take charge of a situation. As parents become aware of the particular "bent" of each child in the family, they can nurture and provide resources for each one to blossom. In adolescence, then, these abilities begin to flower, forming an essential part of the young person's identity.

To the degree a child has internalized these skills and traits, he will have them as resources during the struggles of adolescence. But make no mistake, every young person faces difficulties during the adolescent years. The question "Who am I?" is a painfully difficult one, even for those who have entered this time with a wealth of insight, experience, and stability. And for those who enter these rough waters in a leaky lifeboat and with few supplies, the challenges can be overwhelming. The identity crisis is seen in questions that parallel the skills begun in childhood, now developed more fully in adolescence:

- Who do I belong to? Who cares about me? Who do I love?
- Am I needy or strong? Can I make it on my own?

- If I try new things, will I be condemned if I fail?
- What do I do really well? What about me is admirable?

These difficult and complex questions aren't addressed in a safe, sterile classroom. No, they are wrestled with by young people going through the traumatic upheaval of biological and social storms. Their bodies are changing dramatically, in ways they never have and never will again. Amorphous childhood shapes are transformed into female curves and male muscles. Voices deepen, and hormones surge. Every few months the young person looks in the mirror and wonders, *Who is that?!* Sometimes they like what they see, but far more often, they are frightened or repulsed. Acne, the scourge of adolescence, gnaws on their fragile self-esteem. They see themselves as grotesque monsters. They then look in the mirror and wonder, *What is that?!*

The sociological waves are just as treacherous as the biological ones. Longtime friends drift away, and new people challenge their places in the universe of relationships. Friends become enemies after one simple misunderstanding. Young people desperately want to be included, but the price is often exceptionally high—their sanity, their integrity, or their virginity.

As the child grows through adolescence into adulthood, others have higher expectations of how she should think and act. Teachers and parents expect more responsibility to be evident. The teenager wants this, too, but often feels caught in the middle between the inner desire for freedom and the external demands of others.

In addition, young people begin to see the world with new eyes. They realize that their family isn't like a friend's family—for better or worse. New perception might help them come to the startling realization that things are not what they believed: parents don't love each other as much as they thought, life isn't as safe as they thought, the future isn't as bright as they thought, life is much more confusing and complex than they thought. They become more reflective about their own lives, their failures and successes, their dreams and dreads. Sometimes this generates hope; more often, it produces fear and guilt. As they step into the waters of adulthood and realize they are increasingly on their own, they can become tremendously lonely. All of these new perceptions produce an intense longing for security and love—at the very time the teenager is facing new risks in virtually every arena of life.

I was invited to speak recently to a group of church leaders and pastors about keys to reaching the next generation. I wanted to drive the point home to my audience, who in many ways was out of touch with today's teens. I wanted to do something graphically to give them a picture of this new generation. I took a piece of Plexiglas up to the platform. I had it made so that the Plexiglas was on both sides with a piece of real glass in the middle. It appeared to be one piece of glass. I got a rubber mallet and hit the glass. The inside piece of glass shattered, but the outside Plexiglas kept it from breaking into pieces.

When I held it up, I said: "What you're looking at is a description of an American teenager—smooth on the outside but shattered on the inside. A lot of kids who are smooth on the outside in terms of how they look, but on the inside they're emotionally shattered. One of the many reasons for that is because of broken homes and a lack of love and attention."

By "shattered," I refer to emotional needs that have gone unmet and spiritual and moral confusion; some are even shattered spiritually. Lack of love, attention, and affection, along with fear, despair, instability, and security hurt young hearts. Adults are no different. Many parents today are in the process of raising kids on the fly while they hurry through their lives and professions. Many of them are smooth on the outside but shattered on the inside. Parents are often more sophisticated on the outside than teenagers in how they present themselves. They've done a good job of masking their fears and insecurities by striving to succeed in their careers and buy plenty of material possessions. They think that's what will make life easier and happier, but they're still shattered because they're driven by their insecurities and fears.

It Ain't the Same

Most parents assume their teenagers experience challenges that are very similar to the ones they experienced a generation ago. After all, their music is just as offensive to us as our music was to our parents. The clothes they wear are just as outlandish as ours were. The kinds of trouble kids get into today are just like the trouble we got into. Right? No, things *are* different.

George Barna, the founder and president of the Barna Research Group, observed numerous significant changes in the lives of young people over the past twenty years. These include:

- The dramatic increase in the number of lifestyle choices available to kids.
- The reduction in the number and understanding of moral and ethical absolutes and limitations.
- The quickening of response time in decision making, resulting in spontaneous decisions based on minimal reflection.
- The substantial surge in the volume of information available—quite conveniently and inexpensively—on a vast array of topics.
- The lowered personal standards concurrent to the heightened level of expectations we have of other people and institutions.
- The increase in stress and anxiety along with the decrease of hope and joy.
- The deterioration of the family as a stable base of support.
- The demise of other social institutions focused upon providing support of young people.
- An exceedingly intrusive and opinionated media that passes along its own biases as objective reporting.[1]

Adolescence has always been hard. Now it is even harder for teenagers to navigate those dangerous waters because there are more cultural reefs to smash their boats on and more sharks to bite them.

Red Flags

The stresses in the lives of today's teenagers are enormous, and many of them struggle under the strain. How do you know if the difficulties your teenager experiences are normal or if they are signs of a serious problem? Here are some red flags to watch for:

- difficulty in relationships: fighting, withdrawing, not taking part in normal social activities
- difficulties in school: grades dropping, not interested in anything in the school environment, causing trouble
- changes in eating or sleeping habits
- morbid or self-destructive thoughts: "offhand" comments about wanting to be dead, an obsession with images or music that deals with death, any plans to end life
- hopelessness and lethargy: giving up at school, in sports, or in friendships
- change in friendships: rejecting old friends and finding new friends who are suspected of drug use, promiscuity, etc.; unwillingness to bring new friends home to meet you; secretiveness about activities
- problems with money: stealing, gambling, begging for money from you or siblings and friends
- mood swings: excessive highs and lows, constantly angry at home
- physical problems: difficulty staying awake, chronic headaches or upset stomach, glazed expression
- drug use: owning drug paraphernalia, needle marks, etc.
- blaming others for problems

Some parents go ballistic if they see even the smallest change in their adolescent, but that reaction doesn't give the teenager room to grow. Other parents, however, refuse to see the problem when it is evident to everyone else. If you want to get an objective perspective on how you're responding to your child's behavior, get a third party's perspective. Ask a close friend or relative that spends a lot of time around your child.

Look for patterns, look for significant changes, and look into your teenager's heart to see if hope is there.

Support and Hurdles

A multitude of factors shape a young person's life and either add or detract from his ability to navigate successfully the stormy waters of adolescence. Of course, parental support is the most important. Even though many adults believe peer pressure is the dominant force in the lives of teenagers, recent studies show that parents continue to play the most crucial role. Many years ago, psychologist Virginia Satir observed that parents don't have to be perfect to raise emotionally healthy and responsible children. They just need to be, in her cryptic phrase, "good enough parents," providing enough love, enough boundaries, enough correction, and enough praise. The excesses of too much control or too little involvement are the problems that cause damage. When a parent smothers the child with directions, the child learns, "I'm not competent to make my own decisions. I'd better do what others tell me to do." That may seem to work well when the child is listening only to the parent, but in the teenage years, other voices are heard—and heeded. Or if a parent is emotionally or physically distant, the child believes she isn't worthy of love and attention. Her conclusion is that life isn't safe, so she either tries to win approval through success or sex, or she withdraws so the risk of being hurt again is minimized.

Good friends play a powerful role in the development of young people. All of us can quickly name our best friends from high school. Some of those people influenced us for good; some, in negative ways. But the influence was deep and profound. Earlier in this chapter we looked at the proverb, "He who walks with the wise grows wise." Young people who have responsible friends become responsible themselves; those who hang out with angry people become angry; and those who spend inordinate amounts of time with underachievers rarely rise above their friends.

The skills learned as children are employed as adolescents. Problem solving, thinking and resolving difficulties, "reading" people, and processing emotions are skills children observe in their parents and older brothers and sisters. When they become teenagers, they put these skills to work and refine them for their own use. When these abilities are in the young person's toolkit, he can pull them out whenever they are needed. If, however, the toolkit is empty or the tools are dull and broken, the teenager will have great difficulty constructing new ones in the heat of the moment.

One of the primary windows on the health of a young person is his attitude toward trust. Struggling teenagers demand that their parents and others trust them, but healthy teenagers understand that trust—the most valuable relational commodity—must be earned. They work hard at preserving their integrity by being responsible and responding to correction when they fail—which they, like all of us, will inevitably do.

All of Us Are Changing

In this chapter we have focused on the incredibly complex changes young people experience as they grow from children to adults. They are learning a new way to live as independent men and women who are capable of following their dreams and building lasting relationships with God and with other people. But parents are changing too. Some of us don't get the hang of what's happening until one or two of our children have left the nest, but sooner or later we realize our task as parents is not just to protect and provide but to give these young people a launching pad so they may take off on their own.

Some of us resent the fact that our teens are growing up, and some of us are afraid they'll make the same mistakes we made—or worse. Instead of trying to cling to our children, we need to celebrate their fledgling attempts. Rejoice when they try new things they'll need the rest of their lives, applaud them when they succeed, and encourage them when they fail. The question we have to ask is, What kind of adult do I want my child to become? If the answer is a strong, independent, responsible adult, then we need to begin treating them like that now. They will, in large measure, become what we envision them to be. If we see them as needy and incompetent, that's what they'll be. If we see them as too much trouble, they'll be trouble for themselves and others for years to come. But if we see past their acne and braces, past their dumb decisions and awful clothes, and see instead people who are becoming wonderful and honorable, then they just may grow up to fulfill those dreams.

Disappointed and Angry

For many of us, we hope that our teenagers will become wonderful, responsible adults. We bought this book because we are angry and disappointed. We have tried as hard and as long as we possibly can, and the results aren't looking too good right now. Before we go further, let me suggest three possible reasons for this disillusionment:

The compulsion to control. It is a vicious cycle: the more out of control the teenager is, the more we feel we have to control. The more we control, the more the teenager rebels and is out of control. And on and on and on. This cycle of control and rebellion simply won't take you where you need to go. It only leads to more hurt, despair, and resentment for both of you. We will see in a later chapter that this cycle can be broken by giving your teenager choices and enforcing clear consequences. This takes the burden of his choices off you and puts it squarely where it belongs—on him.

Wrong goals. Let's face it, some of us are just as self-centered as our teenagers. Our goal is primarily to make life as easy as possible for us. If anybody gets in the way (and you can be sure of one thing: your teenager will certainly get in the way!), they become a hindrance to us in achieving our goal. We get angry, really angry. And we feel completely justified because he or she is so selfish and not caring at all about us. Coming face-to-face with our own sinful selfishness isn't pleasant, but for some of us it is absolutely essential. Parenting adolescents takes sacrifice and courage, even in the best of families and with the best of teenagers.

Putting our hope in people. Some of us have prayed and struggled so long with so little success that we have given up on God's working in our teenager's life. Some of us haven't started praying at all. It is easy for us to trust in ourselves to fix our teenager, or to trust in our spouse to come up with the right answers, or to trust in a pastor or a counselor, or even a book, instead of trusting in our sovereign and loving God. Certainly God may use a spouse or counselor or pastor or a book to give us some direction, but our primary source of wisdom and hope is God himself. As we trust him and listen more carefully to him, we may find out that he is just as interested in working in our lives as he is in working in our teenager's life. God wants us to cling to him, and perhaps he is using this difficult time as a classroom to teach us to open our hearts more fully and experience his peace and purpose even in our darkest days.

A Closer Look

1. Is selfishness a necessary part of adolescence? Why or why not?

2. Describe how the following traits are a platform for a young person to develop into a strong, loving, mature adult:
   trust _____
   independence _____
   creativity _____
   expertise _____

3. Describe how the young person might think and act if those same characteristics aren't developed:
   lack of trust _____
   unhealthy dependence _____
   lack of creativity _____
   sense of incompetence _____

4. Look at the list of how things are different today from what they were twenty years ago. Which two or three of these seem most significant to you? Explain.

5. Look at the list of problem signs on page 20. Which of them (if any) can you identify in your teenager?

6. Do any of the characteristics of disappointment and anger (the compulsion to control, wrong goals, and putting our hope in people) apply to you? If so, what are you going to do about it?

THREE

IS HISTORY REPEATING ITSELF?

"I swore I'd never treat my kids the way my mother treated me." The look on Carol's face spoke louder than her words. She was deeply distressed, guilt-ridden, and confused. As she told me her story, she was only one step away from complete hopelessness.

"My dad was a good man—when he was sober and not hung over. But most of the time, he didn't want to get involved in any of the problems in our family. And there were plenty. My mother was just the opposite. She was involved all right. She was (and still is, by the way) a drill sergeant, demanding that my two brothers and I do exactly as she said—immediately! I lived in terror. Oh, on the outside everybody thought we had a wonderful family, but they didn't know what went on when the doors were closed. I have vivid memories, not so much of Dad's drinking, but more of Mother's rage. I can still see the hateful look in her eyes and the venomous glare. She could stare a hole through a brick wall . . . but I wasn't made of brick. One of my brothers became a star athlete in high school. That was his way of getting along. I guess my other brother just couldn't take it. As far back as I can remember, he was a bum. He didn't do well in school. Oh, he was plenty smart, but he didn't try. And beginning in junior high, he drank, sniffed glue, and then began using other drugs. Me? I was the 'good kid.' I tried to do everything I possibly could do to please my mother . . . and keep her from getting mad at me."

Carol continued to talk about her experiences as an adolescent. "When I was in high school, I felt really confused. I wanted to be out on my own, but I sure wasn't willing to cross my mother!" Carol laughed nervously. "No matter what I did, no matter what kind of things I was involved in, in the back of my mind was one question: 'What will Mother think of this?' It's like my mother lived in my head. I didn't have a conscience; I had my mother's voice! At every step, I heard her voice of warning or of condemnation. I could see her eyes roll and her glare if I said or did anything she wouldn't agree with—even if I was sure she'd never know about it!

"My dad didn't want to get involved. He read his paper or walked out of the room when Mom got her anger rolling at us. I think he'd heard enough of it coming his way, and he just couldn't take it. Oh, sometimes when my bum brother did something really stupid, my father would explode at him along with my mother, but after the eruption, the volcano went silent again. Actually"—Carol reflected now—"I can see why my dad acted that way. His own father was one of the meanest people I've ever known. I know I shouldn't say that about my own grandfather, but it's the truth. All my dad's brothers and sisters were afraid of him."

Carol's story then skipped forward a few years to her own marriage. "When my husband and I had children, I swore I'd never treat them the way my mother treated me. But then, when they were toddlers and getting into everything, I'd explode at them and glare at them and demand that they never do it again. I don't know who felt worse at that moment, me or them. I hated myself for hurting them like that. But I couldn't control myself. Things got a little better when the kids were in grade school, but when they got to junior high and high school, the demons came back. I gave them clear rules—very strict rules—about what I expected of them. When they failed, I went ballistic. When they asked for something simple, like to stay out thirty minutes later, I went ballistic too. I felt like they were attacking me! I could see the pain on their faces, and that look crushed me."

Carol reflected on the system she lived in: "I wanted my husband to help, to back me up and tell them what we wanted them to do, but he usually just mumbled something and let them off the hook. Then he'd walk away. After a while, I saw it: my husband was just like my dad, and I was just like my mother! I had married my dad, and I had become my mother! How could that happen? I don't know what to do." Carol hung her head now. "Rodney, can you help me?"

The Necessity of Looking Back

The past doesn't just go away as we get older. Many of us, like Carol, are determined to be better parents than our parents were to us, but we fail. And we hate ourselves for it. We are haunted by the past, and we can't seem to break free. We pray, we read, we make solemn resolutions, but nothing changes. People come to me everywhere I speak to ask questions about how to respond to their teenagers. Some of these parents want tips in "crowd control"; they just want to get the problem over as soon as possible with as little trouble as possible. But some are more honest and more reflective. Their questions center on the issue, What can I do to be a better parent? They are willing to look at themselves and see if they are contributing in any way to the conflict they are enduring with their teenager.

Books are full of techniques about how to do this and how to do that (and this book has some techniques too), but I believe that gaining a clear perception is even more important than learning new skills. If we see clearly, we will know when and how to use those skills. In this chapter we are going to take a look back so we can have more insight about the present. Then we can find new, more productive ways to relate and have a brighter future. Some of us don't want to look back. It's too painful, so we find any rationalization and excuse to avoid it. But I will tell you the truth: Resolving the past is a vital step toward finding a bright path for the future. If we refuse, we are destined to keep repeating the same mistakes, no matter how hard we try to change.

The Scriptures give both precepts and examples of family patterns being repeated generation after generation. Isaac, a passive father, had sons, Jacob and Esau, who fought and connived against each other for position in the family. Jacob's sons hated one of their brothers, Joseph, and wanted to kill him. Instead, they sold him to slavery in Egypt. Years later, David, the indulgent father, was attacked by his son Absalom. The pattern can be seen in almost any narrative in the Bible. One of the most poignant verses in the Bible predicts blessing for generation after generation for those who love and follow God, but it predicts curses and hardship for those who don't. Woven into the Ten Commandments is this verse: "For I, the LORD your God, am a jealous God, punishing the children for the sin of the fathers to the third and fourth generation of those who hate me, but showing love to thousands who love me and keep my commandments" (Exod. 20:5–6). Old patterns of behavior don't die out easily, but they can be changed by courageous believers who commit themselves to starting new patterns of love, righteousness, integrity, and peace.

I believe that the parenting models we see in our childhood are by far the most powerful and influential factors in determining the kind of parents we become. Watching our parents, experiencing their love or anger, nurture or distance, shapes our perspectives and our behavior. Those years are the software that runs our lives and our responses to our spouses and children. If we received "good enough parenting," we learn to be honest, to give and receive love, and to resolve problems to a significant degree. If not, we develop:

- *A lack of confidence.* We lack a relational compass, or worse, we have one that points in the wrong direction. We are unsure of how to establish relationships, and we don't know how to solve problems that inevitably arise in any meaningful relationship. This spills over into our parenting, and we can't figure out how to show love and keep kids under control at the same time. We may read lots of books and go to lots of seminars, but we just don't seem to get it. Each failure is one more nail in the coffin of self-doubt and despair.
- *Fear of not being a good parent.* Some of us are haunted by fear. We didn't see examples of good parenting when we were children, and we're afraid we can't come through for our own kids. In the middle of the night, we wonder what kind of damage we're doing to them, and we wonder what would happen if people found out how bad a parent we really are.
- *Oppressive guilt.* Doubt and fear are breeding grounds for guilt. We know we're doing the wrong things, but we can't seem to find a way to change. We see the look in our children's faces, and we know we are hurting them. We make resolutions to change, and for a while we can control ourselves. But sooner or later the old ways return, and we are yelling or demanding or withdrawing again. And we feel rotten.

Types of Parents

Perhaps the biggest reason it is difficult to be objective about our parents is that we lack objectivity. After all, most of us only lived in one family system, so we have nothing with which to compare it. Sure, we went to neighbors' houses and visited relatives from time to time, but few of us had the courage or insight to evaluate how that family was different from our own. Without that objectivity, what we experienced, no matter how loving or how abusive, seemed "normal." When we believe our experience is normal, we accept it without asking questions; in fact, we deeply resent anyone having the nerve to ask about it! (Like some of you are resenting this chapter right now.)

Let me stop and make one thing very clear: The goal of this reflection is not to blame anyone. Our purpose here is to assign appropriate responsibility. We cannot point the finger at our parents now and say, "It's your fault that I'm not a good parent!" As adults, we are responsible for our behavior today. But we can look back with objectivity and say, "These factors shaped who I am today. I am now responsible to resolve them so they don't impact me and my family negatively any longer." Do you see the difference? Some people are tremendously defensive about their parents. We're not attacking anyone here, but we are trying to shine light on the past so we can make better choices today.

Let's look at parenting types to see which one fits your experience as a child.

Loving, nurturing parents. "Good enough parents" provide stability and affection. The children know they are loved, and they know the parents love each other. It is not, however, the "perfect family." Stresses and disappointments still occur, but they talk about things. In fact, the struggles are stepping-stones for building more trust and good communication. The family knows how to resolve conflict, and it knows how to laugh.

Smothering, overprotective parents. It sometimes looks like love, but smothering is a fear response, not love. Some parents are so afraid that their children will make a mistake, they try to control every aspect of their lives. This may work pretty well when the children are young, but it breaks down terribly during the adolescent years when the teenager wants and needs to learn independence. Some parents smother their kids with a smile and lots of hugs; some do it with dictatorial commands. Either way, the child grows up believing that she isn't competent to make her own decisions. Somebody else has to make them for her.

Distant, withdrawn parents. Some are distant physically, because of death or divorce, and some are distant emotionally. Emotionally distant parents often feel overwhelmed with life, and the only way they know to cope is to stay away from the risk of disappointment and failure in relationships, even those closest to them. Children in these families believe they aren't worthy of love. Even when it is offered, they have difficulty accepting it. Instead, they either withdraw into their own world or try to prove themselves through success.

Demanding, perfectionistic parents. I've seen parents who demanded that their children achieve exceptionally high standards, especially in school. They justify these expectations by saying, "It's for his own good," but it devastates the child who believes he can never quite measure up, no matter how hard he tries and no matter how much he achieves. With every success, the bar is raised just a little higher.

Abusive parents. Abuse takes many forms: verbal, sexual, and physical. All of them are forms of emotional abuse. Children absorb their surroundings and the attitudes of their parents. If they experience abuse, they believe, "There must be something terribly wrong with me. I must be a really bad person." That sense of shame and worthlessness drives the child to find an identity in any way he can, but often the cycle continues generation after generation.

Double messages. If parents were completely consistent, children would have a clearer idea of how to play the game, but quite often children receive double messages from a parent. One lady told me her mother could express rage one minute and then hug her the next. This produces both fear and hope—fear of being hurt again and hope of being loved. Double messages are incredibly manipulative because both fear and hope drive us to do whatever it takes to please that person.

Mixed messages. In many families parents have very opposite ways of relating to the children. In Carol's case, her father was passive, and her mother was domineering. Quite often, divorce creates mixed messages for the children. One parent leaves the home and becomes distant, and the other tries to make up for all the pain by being permissive and indulgent, giving the kids whatever they want. Mixed messages confuse the children and create even more uncertainty. The motive of the indulgent parent may be love, but the result is more damage.

Erosion and Shattering

As I have talked with parents and teenagers over the years about family dynamics, many of them focus on the horrors of physical or sexual abuse. Those who didn't experience these tragedies sometimes comment, "Rodney, my childhood wasn't that bad. My father didn't rape me or anything like that, but I still feel stuck. I can't make sense of things." Some of us experience the erosion of trust, and some experienced shattering experiences. It is easier to identify the shattering traumas such as sexual abuse, though healing from those experiences is a long, difficult journey. Far more of us endured something more difficult to identify—the daily grind of condemnation, demands, or neglect. We can't point to particular moments, to any ax blows of incredible betrayal like the victims of sexual abuse can. Instead, we have to look at the eroding effects of messages such as: "You'll never measure up"; "I knew you'd screw that up"; "Why do you even try?"; "Why can't you be like your sister?"; "Get out of here and leave me alone"; and countless other corrosive statements. Any one or a few of these wouldn't make much of a difference, but when they occur day after day, year after year, the effect is like sanding a board. It takes a long time to sand all the way through, but sooner or later, it is ruined.

One of the most sinister experiences we can endure is what some people call "spiritual abuse." Others call it "toxic faith." When the erosion or shattering of trust occurs in a home that pretends to follow Christ, the child is even further damaged. Carol's grandfather, who was known to his children as the meanest man alive, was a deacon in his church. Another lady told me she was beaten if she failed to memorize perfectly the Bible verses her father assigned to her. When parents tell the world they follow Christ but are devils to their families, the children grow up understandably terrified or angry toward God. When these children grow up and have children of their own, they may respond in kind by demanding that their children obey God and harshly punishing them for any perceived indiscretion. Or conversely, they may react in the opposite way and, out of their own hurt experienced in spiritual matters, condemn their children for any interest they may have in knowing God. Or they may simply withdraw from the spiritual arena altogether, leaving their children with the legacy of spiritual emptiness.

Same Degree, Different Type

You may be reading these descriptions and conclude, "Carol may have realized that she is just like her mother, and other people may be just like their parents, but I'm nothing like mine. So I must not be affected." My answer to that statement is that just as it's impossible to swim in the ocean and not get wet, it's impossible to live in a seriously flawed family and not be damaged in some way. People typically experience the same degree of pathology as their parents, but it may be expressed in completely different ways. For example, someone who had loud and demanding parents may become a passive and indulgent parent. A person who was abandoned and felt lonely much of her life may feel compelled to smother her children with affection and try to be involved (too involved) with every detail of their lives. Some of us are carbon copies of one of our parents, and, like Carol, we have married someone just like our opposite-gender parent. Others of us react by becoming mirror images—our way to cope with stress, pain, and confusion is just the opposite of our parents'. That doesn't make it any better or worse—it's just the truth.

Obviously, we need to bring God into this dilemma, but sadly, I've talked to some parents who bring him in as a condemner, not a healer. As they describe their problems with their teenagers, they have told me things like, "I guess God is punishing me for how I acted when I was a teenager." That kind of conclusion doesn't help. God loves you, and he loves your teenager. He's not in the business of revenge, and he certainly doesn't use the struggles of others to hurt us. A more accurate analysis is probably that the cycle of pain is continuing from generation to generation, and it's up to you to break that cycle now. You are obviously committed to that because you are reading this book and ready to take action. The faith that you are expressing through your prayers and actions pleases God. Be assured of that.

Fear and Triangles

Many parents are consumed by fear, and they interpret struggles with their teenager as a personal attack. After all, the yelling and glares sure seem personal, don't they? Unfortunately, this interpretation lights the fuse that contributes to more hurt, more fear, and more angry reactions. Instead of lighting that fuse by seeing every painful interaction as a personal attack, we need new interpretations. We need to diffuse the bomb by being objective.

One of the ways we try to lower the level of fear, anger, and hurt is by deflecting these emotions to a third person. This is called a triangle. Triangling is so common that most of us don't even realize what we're doing. In fact, it is something that is usually modeled and passed down from generation to generation. It is a destructive coping mechanism because it keeps us from resolving conflict. Here's a definition: a triangle occurs when we attempt to reduce anxiety in one relationship by focusing on a third party who seems safer. Instead of addressing problems directly, we deflect them to a person who is less threatening. For example, a married couple, John and Mary, are having difficulties. They have a daughter in junior high, Susan. When John comes home late because he had a flat tire, Mary yells at him, "How could you be so inconsiderate to Susan?! She was counting on you to take her to her basketball game!"

John replies, "I couldn't help it! If you hadn't driven in that new subdivision with your friends to show them that house last night, I wouldn't have gotten a nail in my tire." Then he looks at his daughter, "And besides, Susan probably wasn't ready anyway." He then spits out at Susan, "You're never ready when you need to go somewhere." Then back to Mary, "That's your job to make sure she's ready. Why is it always my fault when she doesn't get somewhere?"

Do you see what's going on here? Instead of addressing the problem in their marriage, Mary blamed John for being inconsiderate to Susan. Was she upset for Susan's sake? Probably not much, if at all. Her anger boiled up because she felt John had been inconsiderate to her many times, but it felt safer for her to blame John for being rude to Susan. In the same way, John refused to address the long-simmering marriage problem. Instead, he blamed Mary for the flat tire that caused him to be late, and he blamed Susan for not being ready, even though he had no way of knowing whether she was ready or not. So here's the scorecard:

- Mary presents the problem as between John and Susan. (John was inconsiderate and failed to take Susan to the game.)
- John presents the problem as between Mary and Susan. (Mary needs to be sure to get Susan ready so John doesn't have be bothered.)

- And Susan? She can work both sides of the fence. When her mother is angry with her, she can go to her dad and complain; and when her dad is angry with her, she can complain to her mother.

Being late, the flat tire, Susan being ready on time—those aren't the real problems in this marriage. It would be much more productive for all concerned if one of the parents would say, "You know, we need to talk about us. I'm feeling hurt and angry, and I want us to have a better relationship. These other things—they are tangents. We need to talk about you and me, not those things." Honesty is more productive, but it also involves the risk that the other person will say, "Yes, and you are the problem. I'm leaving." Still, the risk of not addressing the real problem is that the marriage will continue to drift toward irreconcilable bitterness and, possibly, divorce. Another risk is that the parents are teaching and modeling a destructive "dance" that Susan will almost certainly dance with her husband and children in a few years. Both ways of relating involve risks, but only one has a genuine reward.

Triangles are, ultimately, dishonesty about needs and responsibility. Instead of speaking the truth to those whom we need and who have hurt us, we involve someone else—often a child, but it can be anyone at work, at home, or in our network of relationships. We express our hurt, fear, and anger, but we deflect it to a secondary issue, not the one that desperately needs addressing. We hope other people will play along, and they usually will. As stated before, the use of triangles is passed down from generation to generation. If you saw this phenomenon in your relationship with your parents and siblings, the model is set—and it is strong. It is entirely likely that you are following that same pattern of deflecting tension, anger, and hurt to someone else so that you can avoid addressing the real problem in your life.

INEFFECTIVE SOLUTIONS

Just as pain and anger are passed down in various forms from generation to generation, ineffective solutions are modeled and acquired as well. Even though they don't work, and even though we despised it when our parents used them on us, we still continue to use them. Here are some that many parents use:

Demands for compliance. Instead of giving someone choices and consequences, the freedom to make decisions, and the accountability for them, some parents demand compliance to their rigid (but sometimes changing) rules. This destructive discipline alienates the teenager and robs her of her choice. Harsh and arbitrary punishments cause further damage to the individual and the relationship.

Pep talks. This is a favorite of some parents who think that if they just say the right thing, their teenager will suddenly and magically change into Prince or Princess Charming. If they can just say it with enough passion, or with the right metaphor, or using the most juicy personal story, surely that will work. But the kids have heard it before—many times before—so they tune out before the first line is uttered. Because pep talks are usually long on enthusiasm and short on consequences, there is no real motivating factor (like losing use of the car for a week) to encourage a change in behavior.

Neglect. "Give it time. It'll change." Some parents think that neglecting a problem will somehow cause it to evaporate. But neglecting a festering wound only allows time for the infection to spread.

Distance. The "solution of choice" for passive people is simply to get away from the person. If that's not possible, then simply avoid talking about the problem. This solution has short-term benefits and long-term liabilities. It avoids the tension of facing the facts, but it also avoids the possibility of honesty, repentance, restoration, and growth.

Fixing the situation, not the heart. Some parents are energetic and enthusiastic about solving their teenager's problems. Their goal is to be a hero, so they dive in to every difficulty their teenager tells them about (and some they don't) and try to fix it. Their intentions may (or may not) be honorable, but this solution is ultimately destructive for the teenager who needs to learn to deal with life instead of having someone bail her out. This superficial solution also focuses on the circumstance and neglects the heart. Its goal is avoiding pain, not building character.

Hard Reflection

Were these patterns of behavior, triangles, and ineffective solutions evident in your life when you were growing up? Are you repeating them or repeating a mirror image of how your parents treated you? As I have spent time with mothers and fathers during the past few years, I have seen some courageous ones who have looked inside their hearts, reflected on how their parents treated them, and grown tremendously in the process. It is not an easy task, but it can be a way of wonderful healing, hope, and joy as you take steps down that road. Does it seem overwhelming? Are the memories too painful? I've known people with terrible stories who have found genuine grace through the power of the Holy Spirit and the support of committed, loving believers.

A friend of mine, the father of two teenagers, recently told me that he marvels at how God has given him a far more healthy relationship with his wife and children than he would have dared hope for twenty years ago. The only models he experienced as a child were a broken marriage between his parents, bitterness, manipulation, and guilt. Not exactly good soil for emotional and spiritual health! Today, however, he enjoys wonderful honesty and warmth in his family's relationships, and he is grateful daily for God's grace. How did it happen? It came about through a long and painful process of uncovering the ugly truth, grieving the losses of love and trust in crucial childhood relationships, and rebuilding his own identity and the skills to give and receive love. "It wasn't magic," he told me. "It was hard work . . . hard work to learn to trust God for strength to face reality and make concrete changes in how I see myself, how I interpret people's words and circumstances, and how to respond in grace and truth instead of manipulating to get my own way.

"I was honest with my children along the way. That made a huge difference. I let them know that I was working on some deep hurts I had experienced in my own childhood, and my honesty opened doors for some incredible talks among us. And it brought healing. As I experienced grace, love, and truth in new and deeper ways, I asked my kids to do me a favor. I asked them to tell me any time I acted like I used to—angry and manipulative. To their great credit, they have done just that. They have stopped me in the middle of me acting like my father acted and said, 'Dad, you're doing it again.' That honesty provided me with a big dose of reality, and it gave us opportunities to talk about the real issues, not just surface issues. God has worked a miracle in my family. Looking at what I experienced when I was a kid, nobody would have predicted that my relationship with my wife and children could ever be so good; but it is. In fact, my children are far more emotionally and spiritually healthy than I could ever have imagined children of mine could be. It sure didn't happen overnight, and it didn't happen without a lot of struggle and pain. But it happened. And I am tremendously grateful. I thank God every day for these precious people. God has broken the cycle of messed-up generations."

If my friend can experience this kind of healing, so can you.

Sometimes we don't develop this insight until after our children are grown. I received a phone call from a father who heard me speak at a church he attends in Baton Rouge, Louisiana. He shared how he had divorced his wife when his son was in his early twenties. His son got married, but he, too, went through a divorce. The father explained how his divorce had caused division between him and his son, and as a result, his son has had no contact with his father.

Although the father has made numerous efforts to reconcile with his son through phone calls, letters, and gifts, the son has never responded to his dad. This has devastated the father, who desperately wants to make things right with his son.

The father called me wanting advice. He said he was thinking about buying a ticket to Houston to show up unexpectedly and visit his son. I told him if he thought it would give him peace of mind to know that he had exhausted every possible means, then he should go. If he goes uninvited, however, he shouldn't expect a warm welcome. The son still felt the dad was the reason for all the family's problems. (Divorce makes people take sides. It is like an open wound that never heals. It creates complications in every relationship.) The dad felt that he had to try one more time, so he got on a plane and went searching for his son, in hopes to make peace between them.

Each person needs to realize he should never justify his wrong behavior and disobedience because someone else has made a mistake. That's no excuse. We are each responsible for our choices, no matter what the circumstances. Parents should do all they can to show unconditional love and acceptance to their kids. They may not accept the teenager's poor behavior, but they can accept their child as a person. Never give up hope in what God can do to bring healing to the situation. Scripture says, "Greater is He who is in you than he who is in the world" (1 John 4:4 NASB). God will empower us to be obedient to what God has called us to do as parents. When we have done all we can do, we have to let go and let God take over. That doesn't mean we stop being parents, but we quit trying to force something good to happen. Sometimes a teenager has to learn tough lessons in order for him to respond to God.

We can't change the past, but we can change how we approach our future. We do not have to continue to relate to one another in unhealthy, negative, destructive patterns that have plagued the family for years, or even for generations. Second Corinthians 5:17 states, "Old things are passed away; behold, all things are become new" (KJV). God is in the business of creating new beginnings through forgiveness and the love of Christ. As a result, parents can have the luxury of establishing a new family legacy of love and strength. This should be done early in life when children are small. Establishing new habits does not serve as a guarantee, but they diminish the chances of kids destroying their lives and causing grief for the parents.

Some parents tell me they've done everything they know to do and have tried everything they know to try, but for whatever reason, their son or daughter has chosen to rebel. I want to tell you, God is still a God of miracles. Sometimes those miracles are first worked in the parents to produce a new, stronger faith where there has been doubt and despair.

A Closer Look

1. Describe your parents' relationship with each other.
   - How did they show affection?
   - How did they resolve conflict?
   - What did they enjoy about each other?
   - How did they handle money, in-laws, sex, and child raising?
   - What were the important events in their relationship? How was the relationship affected by each event?

2. Describe your relationship with your mother.
   - How did she show affection to you?
   - How did she correct you?
   - Describe some times you enjoyed being with her.
   - In what ways is your parenting style like or unlike hers?

3. Describe your relationship with your father.
   - How did he show affection to you?
   - How did he correct you?

- Describe some times you enjoyed being with him.
- In what ways is your parenting style like or unlike his?

4. Describe your relationship with your siblings.
   - What are some warm and fun memories?
   - What are some painful memories?
   - Did your parents treat all the children the same or differently? Explain.

5. What types of recurring conflict did your family experience? What attempts were made to resolve them?

6. On a scale of 0 (never) to 10 (all day, every day), rate how often you experienced the following from your parents and siblings. (You may want to make a separate mark for each person in the family.)

Trust

0————————————5————————————10

Love

0————————————5————————————10

Affirming words

0————————————5————————————10

Warm, caring touch

0————————————5————————————10

Encouragement for the future

0————————————5————————————10

Conflict resolution

0————————————5————————————10

Joy

0————————————5————————————10

Compassion
0————————————5————————————10

Fairness
0————————————5————————————10

Protection
0————————————5————————————10

Demands
0————————————5————————————10

Distancing
0————————————5————————————10

Rage
0————————————5————————————10

Unreasonableness
0————————————5————————————10

Unpredictability
0————————————5————————————10

What stands out to you as you look at these scores? Explain.

7. Now chart your current relationship with your spouse and children. (Make a different mark for each person.)

Trust
0————————————5————————————10

Love
0————————————5————————————10

Affirming words
0————————————5————————————10

Warm, caring touch
0————————————5————————————10

Encouragement for the future
0————————————5————————————10

Conflict resolution

0————————5————————————10

Joy

0————————5————————————10

Compassion

0————————5————————————10

Fairness

0————————5————————————10

Protection

0————————5————————————10

Demands

0————————5————————————10

Distancing

0————————5————————————10

Rage

0————————5————————————10

Unreasonableness

0————————5————————————10

Unpredictability

0————————5————————————10

What stands out to you as you look at these scores? Explain.

8. What impact has your relationship with your parents had on
   - your hopes?
   - your fears?
   - the way you give and receive love?
   - the way you handle conflict?
   - your relationship with your spouse?
   - your relationship with your children?
   - your relationship with God?

FOUR

HOW MUCH IS TOO MUCH?

One of the most bizarre situations I ever encountered occurred between a man, his wife, and their two daughters. The couple had been married for many years, and both daughters were in their middle to late teens when the mother and father began experiencing major marital problems. The mother confessed that she was having a lesbian affair. During this time of separation and divorce proceedings, the father also had an affair.

The daughters were devastated when they discovered the behavior of their mom and dad. Less than a year after the divorce was final, the father remarried a girl half his age. In fact, his new wife wasn't much older than his oldest daughter. The new bride soon got pregnant, and they had a daughter. The father now was living in a new home with a new wife, a new baby, and two almost-grown daughters.

When the older daughter went away to college, the younger daughter was still living at home with her father, although she no longer had a relationship with him. She was angry, extremely bitter, and defiant because of all that had happened. Her dad tried to make life easy for her by giving her nice things—a new car and anything she wanted. As a result, there was no accountability. She hung out with the wrong crowd because that was the only way she felt she could get any kind of acceptance. She certainly felt that she wasn't getting any attention at home. The focus of her dad and stepmom was on that little baby. The older sister was not only in college; she also got plenty of attention because she was in beauty pageants. So this middle child didn't fit into the equation of love and affection. She felt left alone, isolated. Her attitude was, "Since no one else cares, why should I?"

She started hanging out at grocery store parking lots with friends, sitting on the hoods of their cars until late at night. She went to parties, drank heavily, and used drugs. She dabbled with cocaine and soon became addicted. To get coke from her dealer, she often drove alone to downtown Dallas at 2:00 A.M. She was risking her life to get drugs.

She continued her downward spiral and lost a lot of weight. My wife and I lived across the street from this family, and we knew something was wrong. We became concerned because we saw a beautiful young woman begin to self-destruct. Her cycle of increased drug use continued until she eventually overdosed and had to be rushed to the hospital. Her family asked me to visit her. As I sat by her bedside that day, I saw a beautiful girl in an extreme amount of emotional pain. She was the victim of a family who had gone through tragic transition, and drug use was the only way she knew to cope with her pain. Her quest for recognition and attention quickly became a downward spiral in her life—spiritually, emotionally, and physically.

When she came out of the hospital, the family was at wit's end with her. They'd done everything they knew to do. She was having knock-down, drag-out fights with her stepmom. They hated each other and fought over everything. The father tried to be the peacemaker, but he soon joined the yelling matches. The relationship at home was so depressing and destructive, she had to get out of there.

The family came to me for suggestions. I said, "First of all, before we can get genuine help and bring healing to the situation, she must be willing to get help. We can give suggestions all day long, but until she reaches the point where she's willing to let go and let God take over, and stop doing what she's doing, we can't get her help." We had a meeting with her, and I confronted her to determine if she was ready to get help. She said she was. I then began looking for different places for her to live.

The girl didn't want to go live with her mother because of the mother's lifestyle. I finally found a place she was willing to go, a home for teenage addicts and delinquent kids in the Tennessee mountains. This girl began to get a reality check. She began to realize that many of the girls in this environment had gone through the same problems for the same reasons. They, too, wanted to be loved, to find acceptance. This Christian-based outreach and ministry created an environment of unconditional love and acceptance for these girls and taught them to see themselves as loved and valuable, yet responsible and accountable.

A wonderful healing process began in this girl's life. After being away for nearly three months, she made a complete, 180-degree turnaround in her life and was finally ready to reenter the world as a changed person. Unfortunately, the family was still going through the same crazy, mixed-up problems at home. When the time came for her to get out of the treatment facility, the question was, Would it be the best thing for her to move back home? By now the girl was seventeen and going into her senior year in high school. She moved back home and tried to make things work with her family. Yet there was still underlying tension in her relationship with the stepmother, who resented the problems she had created by her drug use. She and her husband, however, had a plan to solve the problem.

This was a religious family. In fact, very religious. The father believed his daughter's addiction was the product of demonic activity, so he determined to cast them out. He asked some friends to come to the house and sprinkle the door with oil. They prayed and claimed victory as they walked into the daughter's bedroom casting out demons and rebuking Satan. They went to extreme spiritual measures to get this girl set straight, but they neglected to love her.

All she ever wanted was to be loved and accepted. My wife and I had her over for dinner by herself during the Christmas holidays. We talked for several hours and reflected back on all that she'd been through. She told us she had learned a lot and had grown and had gotten her life back together. We asked her what drove her to the point of almost taking her life by overdosing on a lethal drug? As we talked, she told us that all she ever wanted in her life was to be loved by her father.

By this time the father and stepmother were pregnant with their second child. This middle daughter still felt alone, isolated, unloved, and unwanted. She believed she was a nuisance. Her real mother was a permissive parent, so she was looking for structure in her life. She wasn't getting it from her dad because he gave her whatever she wanted just to get her out of the house. The older sister was popular at school, beautiful, talented, involved in the Miss Texas pageants, and always getting exposure and attention for her accomplishments. The father put his oldest daughter on a pedestal. A new dynamic was created with the half sisters who were now in the picture. This beautiful young woman had no identity.

The father should have taken more responsibility for being a leader of his home. He also should have taken responsibility for his sin of having an affair and asked forgiveness from his daughters. But he never did. His bad example and hard heart brought much hurt and confusion. If he had confessed his sin and tried to make every wrong right in the eyes of his family, if he had been a spiritual leader to gather the family together and mend the hurt, he could have at least created a better environment and established a better foundation for his new family to build upon.

It would have been beneficial if he had taken a weekend retreat with his two daughters to spend time together and talk through the past before he remarried. He could have prepared them for what was ahead and tried to work together as a family to see what new ground rules they could establish so they could relate to each other as the new stepmother came into the picture. He could have helped them define roles and expectations, as well as help them cope with all the new dynamics and changes that were about to be placed on the family instead of letting it be sprung on them. This essential process of communication would have reinforced his love to his daughters. If he had let them know that no matter what happens, his love and affection for them could never change, his family could have remained a family. Let this story remind us as parents to never assume our kids will understand the inconsistencies of our actions. We must allow conflict and change to produce doorways for understanding and acceptance. Don't wait until tragedy strikes or a loved one hits rock bottom before we recognize their needs. It's better to be proactive in our relationships rather than reactive.

Conflict can be a natural, normal part of the parent-teen relationship. Even so, there comes a point when conflict is unhealthy. Parents need to recognize the warning signs so they can take appropriate action. Sometimes, however, a big part of the problem is the parents' interpretation. A wrong evaluation makes things worse than they really are. If hurt feelings, misunderstanding, and unresolved anger are left unaddressed and unresolved, the relationship between parents and teens can self-destruct. It is crucial for parents to know how much conflict is too much so they can turn a negative situation into a positive resolution before it's too late.

When we take a closer look, we need to be ruthlessly honest about what we find. We may see that the problem is squarely our teenager's bad behavior, or we may realize we are contributing to the problem in a significant way. There may also be some stresses that add pressure to both sides. Whatever the problem's source, we need a fresh touch of God to give us wisdom and strength.

In my experience and observation, real problems occur when parents go too far on either end of the continuum of trust and control. If they try to control too rigidly, even little conflicts become World War III. If they are too passive, the young person is left without a moral compass and wanders into deep and destructive waters. The situation is complicated even further because these two extremes are often married to each other! The teenager then gets powerfully conflicting messages from powerfully conflicting parents.

As we take a closer look at how much is too much, we will use the metaphor of a traffic light: red is for real problems, yellow signifies caution, and green means things are going well. Let's take a look at the responsibility for conflict.

Sometimes It's Them

A small percentage of parents come to me with a very specific situation or problem. In most cases parents want to know how to handle their teenager's general attitude. Disrespect is a common attitude problem I hear about from both parents and schoolteachers. Many teachers say that in all their years of teaching, they have never before seen such a widespread problem of disrespect for authority in the classroom as they see today. Kids have an attitude that Mom and Dad are always on their case, so they roll their eyes and sigh at the slightest provocation. Parents want to know what to do because they realize that disrespect is a problem that leads to more problems.

Many factors in our society today add fuel to the fire of the overall attitude of disrespect. Television dramas, movies, sitcoms, MTV, music videos, and the music kids listen to all show defiance, disrespect, and rebellion. Teenagers demand, "I have rights. I can be who I want to be. I don't have to answer to anybody. I'm free to choose."

Kids today think they have a right to do what they want to do, live the way they want to live, and not have to submit to any kind of authority. In fact, a growing percentage of kids in the Christian community also express this defiant, self-centered attitude.

When kids show disrespect to their parents, they're not respecting friends and other members of the family either. Their selfishness provokes anger. If parents fight fire with fire by letting their anger and emotions rule, they will lose the battle almost before it begins. Many parents expect, and even demand, that their teenager respond in complete compliance. They ask their kids repeatedly to help around the house, clean up their rooms, or turn down their music, but they get defiance or apathy in return.

I let the parents know that challenging authority is a common behavior among teenagers because they're exploring their freedom and wanting to gain more and more independence. They want to be out from under Mom and Dad's thumb, and this is a normal and natural tendency—to an extent. Parents still need to enforce respect. They need to be strong in holding their ground and staying true to their convictions. If parents believe it is wrong to be disrespectful to those in authority, they must make that clear to the teenager by explaining the reasons behind their convictions.

If the teenager shows an attitude of defiance—for example, rolling their eyes—a parent should not let it pass. He needs to ask what the reason was behind the action. If the mother is hurt or offended by the act, she should let the teenager know so he understands how it makes her feel. At the same time, it's important for the teenager to communicate to the parents why he rolled his eyes. If Mom and Dad are nagging about the same old issue, and he knows what he's supposed to be doing, the teenager should speak the truth about the nagging. Of course, sometimes in the heat of the moment, speaking the truth is very hard. It may be wise to wait a while until things cool down a bit. If you say something every time a child rolls his eyes, it may not be productive. Pick your spots, and speak clearly. Look for patterns and talk about it after a few days. Be sure to talk about what's underneath the disrespect. You may learn that something is going on in the family that is making it difficult to be honest and respectful, and maybe all of you need to change a bit.

When we look at the full spectrum of teenage experience and attitudes, we see that it is entirely normal and healthy to experiment with new ideas. Unmet needs and poor coping skills, however, lead some down a dark path. Let's look at the "lights" that signal how a teenager is coping with life.

Green Light

Disagreeing is not a problem. Asking hard questions is not a sign of rebellion. Teenagers are experimenting with life, and that includes the important issues of trust, authority, and control. Throughout history, and especially in the last fifty years, young people have questioned authority. They want to know that what they've been taught by their teachers and parents will hold water. The questions aren't wrong, and they aren't attacks. They are attempts by these young people to think through fundamental issues on their own and come to their own conclusions. (To be honest, they are asking the same questions you and I asked a few years ago.) They may ask questions about what you believe and challenge your values. That's great! It will make for some wonderful discussions as long as you aren't threatened by them.

A friend of mine who is a pastor was eating dinner with his family when his teenage son said, "There are an awful lot of people who are Hindus and Buddhists and Muslims. And they seem pretty sure of themselves. How can we be sure we're right?" Some fathers, and especially some pastors, would have quickly corrected the boy's thinking, but this dad had a different agenda: he wanted to help his son think through things on his own. He replied, "You're right. They do seem very convinced they're right. I wonder what that's about. What do you think?" This led to a wonderful discussion. In fact, it led to lots of meaningful discussions about world religion, personal faith, the validity of Scripture, and a host of other topics. This wise father didn't simply give answers. He mostly asked questions.

Young people's good and healthy experimentation doesn't always end with words and questions. They may color their hair and wear strange clothes. One mother I know draws the line at tattoos. Body piercings can be pulled out and the hole will heal, but tattoos . . .

Yellow Light

Significant changes in the life of a teenager are a yellow light for parents—changes in eating or sleeping habits, the choice of friends, school performance, interest in sports or clubs, and moods. Almost all teenagers are moody, but wide and rapid mood swings may be a sign of trouble.

It is important to look for patterns. It isn't a big deal that your teenager misses an occasional meal or has a new friend, but losing or gaining significant amounts of weight or hanging out exclusively with kids who have questionable reputations should give you reason to be concerned.

Another yellow light is one many parents fail to recognize. If a child becomes too compliant, it can be a sign she is living in fear. The fear of rejection and deep need to receive approval or acceptance can cause a teen to act out through defiant behavior. They may also show signs of "perfectionism" because of fears or insecurities. Failing to live up to their own unrealistic expectations can cause them to show signs of anger or even withdrawal. Keep in mind that this type of behavior can still be viewed as defiant. Usually defiance is just the symptom of the root problem in one's life. The key is putting your finger on what the root problem is in your son or daughter's behavior.

Speaking of defiant behavior, try to discern the difference between healthy challenges to authority and genuine defiance. Even healthy challenges can have a bit of an "edge" to them. Defiant teenagers on the other hand refuse to listen and are quick to blame and walk away. One angry outburst is not a symptom of a teenager gone wrong, but several weeks or months of strained conversation, uncontrolled anger, and an unwillingness to talk about real issues is a flag you need to recognize.

Behaviors and attitudes in the yellow range may not stay that way. A teenager hanging out with the wrong crowd may simply be a step away from significant trouble. It's time to take action before he takes any more steps down that path.

Red Light

When you see criminal and destructive behavior, the problem is already deep and profound. Doing drugs, selling drugs, gang activity, stealing, chronic fighting, self-destructive behavior—such as self-mutilation, running away, and possession of weapons that aren't used for recreational hunting—are sure signs that you need to get involved.

By this time the teenager is entrenched in a circle of friendships that egg him on. No matter how much he does, the law of diminishing returns keeps him thirsty for more. Alcohol gives way to hard drugs; the need for money to feed his habit prompts him to steal; to get money more easily, he starts selling drugs or gambling; and at each step, the kind of people he is with are more and more defiant and deviant.

I was approached by a grandfather one evening at a church when I was speaking in Lubbock, Texas. The grandfather pulled out of his pocket a newspaper clipping about his granddaughter. He told me his granddaughter's destiny was in the hands of the courts, and he was waiting to see how she was going to be punished. He asked me for prayer. I asked him to tell me her story . . . the whole story.

This grandfather's daughter had married a man and given birth to this little girl. When the girl was in her early teens, the parents got divorced. The mom then lived in a two-bedroom apartment with her daughter and was working to make ends meet. The girl began to rebel because of the hurt, anger, and devastation of her parents' divorce and the painful adjustment of living in a single-parent home. The relationship between her and her mom was tense and angry. The mom was trying to enforce boundaries and share responsibilities around the apartment. She was putting in long hours at work, and when she came home, dinner was supposed to be fixed or clothes washed and folded. She was tired, and she expected her daughter to help with the household chores. Instead, the girl was defiant and refused to help. She blamed her mom for the divorce, and as a result, the girl lost all respect for her mother. She saw her father as the "good guy" because he was passive. He let the girl do whatever she wanted to do. The mom was suddenly trying to be both mom and dad and enforce accountability and responsibility. Tension, yelling, and defiance were the elements of their ongoing, daily conflict. Neither one was willing to budge.

One day the mother came home unexpectedly and found the girl on the couch, naked with her boyfriend. The mother told the boy to get his clothes on and leave. Her daughter went ballistic! She screamed, "How dare you invade my privacy? How dare you treat my boyfriend that way? How dare you walk in being bossy and telling everybody what to do and where to go?"

Late that night when the mom was in bed asleep, the girl got a gun and walked into her mother's bedroom. She put the gun to her mom's head and pulled the trigger. Neighbors called the police. When they entered the apartment, they found the mother dead and the daughter sitting calmly in the living room.

When I met the grandfather who told me this story, this girl had been convicted of murder and was in jail waiting to be sentenced.

Another red light is severe depression in a teenager. Some are not defiant at all; they are numb. They have given up hope, and they drift from home to school with very low motivation and low energy. These are kids at risk just as much as those who are dealing drugs or vandalizing cars, but because they don't make as many headlines, they are easier to ignore. The red light warning signs are by no means a helpless or hopeless situation. I have met countless youth and adults who were once trapped in this lifestyle or behavior. This is where the power of a praying parent and friends can make the difference in a son or daughter's life. At the same time, consequences for this type of behavior might have to run its course. For when many people, especially youth, hit rock bottom they have nowhere to go but up.

If you have a loved one who is traveling down this path, don't give up. Don't turn your back. They need to know no matter what they do or how bad they hurt you, you still love them unconditionally. I will share more thoughts and offer words of hope and healing as I talk about my own family later in chapter 11.

Sometimes It's Us

I've known families in which the teenager was coping very well with the stresses of adolescence, but the parents were basket cases! Let's look at the "lights" in parents' experience.

Green Light

Parents who are doing well are active and involved in their teenagers' lives, while allowing plenty of room for the young person to make their own decisions. These parents give rules and enforce them consistently and fairly, always with appropriate consequences for missteps. When they see a problem, they address it without becoming frantic or trying to fix it for the teenager. They enjoy open communication, and they are quick to admit when they don't know something or when they've made a mistake. They communicate without condemnation and without high control, and this provides the opportunity to resolve problems instead of letting them fester.

Successful parents define responsibilities, continually redefining them as their children grow. Gradually, they turn more and more of the decision making over to their children so the teenager is ready and able to enjoy independence when she goes to college, gets married, or enters the business world.

Yellow Light

Parents who are either obsessed with their teenagers' lives or are uninvolved create problems for young people. With some, everything is a big deal; with others, nothing is a big deal. Either extreme is costly and destructive. Those who are obsessed demand to know about everything the young person is thinking and doing. They worry about what the kid is involved in and what might go wrong. This hypervigilance communicates that the young person can't make his own decisions, and that robs him of confidence. The parent points to the teenager's past failures as proof that he needs her help to survive.

Other parents aren't obsessed with their teenager's problems; they're obsessed with their own. They worry, but not about their child. The focus of their lives is squarely on their own hurts and needs; the needs of others are neglected. Some endure a difficult marriage, but instead of resolving the problem, they brood about it constantly. Others are absorbed by problems at work, the lack of enough money to pay the bills, in-laws, failing health, or unfulfilled sexual desires. Worry, blame, and bitterness cloud their thoughts. Why don't they seek resolution? They remain stuck in this morass because bitterness gives them two important things: identity and energy. They can identify themselves as "the one who was wronged," and they wake up every day energized by thoughts of revenge or of proving to everybody they're successful after all.

Another caution light is when parents are inconsistent in discipline. Although one parent may administer consequences one way one time and another way the next, more often kids experience inconsistent discipline because of a power play between conflicted spouses or ex-spouses. The typical scenario is that one plays the heavy and the other plays the compassionate role. The heavy insists on "making the punishment fit the crime," but the other parent fights for leniency as a way of winning the affection and appreciation of the offending teenager. When one parent isn't around, the other has his way. In any case, the teenager hopes to avoid consequences by appealing to the "kind" parent. The division between the parents deepens, the wayward teen believes he can avoid consequences if he plays his cards right, and nobody wins.

Red Light

The extreme perspectives of being obsessed or being uninvolved can lead to disastrous behaviors. The compulsion to control others creates tremendous internal tension and stress in each relationship. Most of us can contain it for a while, but sooner or later that tension explodes in rage. We yell, we scream, we curse, we hit and throw things. We hurt the people we love most, and we feel awful about it.

In most cases, and especially for conscientious Christian parents, this rage leads to deep feelings of shame and self-condemnation. We conclude that if we feel bad enough for long enough, we can somehow pay for what we've done. Unfortunately, that kind of penance never works. Because it doesn't address the root problems, in a few days or weeks we must do it all over again.

I've known parents to explode repeatedly for several years, then implode in depression. Their anger, hurt, and resentment begin to eat them alive. They simply cannot take the stress of all the unresolved problems, and they give up. Hope is a distant dream, but failure haunts every moment.

Others give up before they become depressed. Perhaps the way they saw their parents deal with difficulties was to walk out and slam the door, so that's the model they follow. After a while, they can't even find the door. They neglect not only the problem but the person. Facing reality is too painful to bear, so they leave their children on their own to figure out life by themselves.

Much of the difficulty for parents in the red zone is that their perspective has become muddied. They interpret normal teenage questions and experimentation as tragic flaws that must be condemned and corrected, and they interpret genuine problems as insurmountable tragedies. Their blood pressure rises with their tone of voice, and instead of resolving these difficulties, they multiply them.

Additional Stresses

Remember, our goal is not to blame anyone. It is to assign appropriate responsibility so we can take action to resolve problems. In most cases, responsibility is not black-and-white, and both parents and the teenager contribute to the conflict. In the vast majority of cases, the tension each feels is made worse by extenuating circumstances totally out of their control. These circumstances are not excuses for sin and bad choices, but understanding them is a step in understanding our reactions and our teenager's reactions.

Several studies have been made on the level of stress caused by events, even good events, in our lives. One of these, the Survey of Recent Events[1] gave a numeric rating to a wide range of things that can happen to us. For example, the one rated the most traumatic is the death of a spouse, with 100 points. A pregnancy rated 40 points, and being fired scored 47. Positive events are also stress producing: marriage was a 50, and Christmas scored 12 points. Some other events that produce stress are:

- divorce
- separation

- health problems
- problems with in-laws
- sexual problems
- financial difficulties or a windfall
- beginning or ending a job
- incarceration
- death of a friend
- a personal achievement
- moving to a new home
- vacation
- trouble with a boss at work
- change in school

There are many others, but this short list illustrates the fact that life's events are stress inducing. The particular scoring isn't as important as the acknowledgment that these things complicate, confuse, and distort our hearts and relationships. They contribute in a significant way to the stress we feel, and multiplied stresses make it even more difficult to respond appropriately to each one individually.

So, What Is God Up To?

Over and over, I have heard distraught parents complain, "Why did God let my son get into drugs?" or "Why did God allow my teenage daughter to get pregnant?" or a hundred other similar questions. These questions ultimately aren't answered, and that further divides hearts from God. The answer is: people are sinful and we make bad decisions. God isn't surprised by the problems we encounter, but he didn't cause them. He gives us the incredible privilege of making choices, as well as the heavy responsibility to live with the consequences. When we blame God for not changing these consequences, we misunderstand him, and we confuse ourselves.

In some of our churches, we hear about the "abundant life," and we believe it is God's guarantee to give us blessings beyond our wildest imaginations. God has, indeed, promised us blessings, but some of those blessings are peace in the midst of struggle, strength to endure hardship, and wisdom to make better decisions. He never promised an easy life. If our model is Jesus, then we can expect to be misunderstood, rejected, and betrayed, all the while knowing we are doing the Father's will. Now that's the abundant life!

A more accurate model of the Christian experience is John Bunyon's classic *Pilgrim's Progress*. In this allegory, the main character, Christian, finds salvation and sets off on his path of spiritual experience. He encounters every imaginable difficulty: discouragement, depression, and disappointment. At one point, his only remaining companion falls into the Slough of Despond and sinks. Christian is all alone, but he keeps going. He doubts and often feels like God abandons him, but he never completely gives up. His one redeeming quality is the faith to take the next step. Struggle, for Christian, is normal. I believe it is normal for us too. When we listen to those who exaggerate the promises of God to make us believe the Christian experience is all cake and ice cream, we become bitterly disillusioned when the dream dies. And it will die. Jesus told his followers, "In this world you will have trouble" (John 16:33). That's his promise! If the men and women of faith—Job, Abraham, Joseph, Daniel, Jeremiah, and the rest—experienced great tests of faith, we shouldn't be surprised that God takes us through some difficulties to test our faith too.

Too often, today's Christians have a "vending machine faith." We think that if we pull the right levers, blessings will pop out. We pray, we serve, we go to church, we give up smoking or cursing, and we are nice to our spouse or coworker because we hope God will perform his magic and give us what we want. I believe God's ways are far higher than that. A vending machine faith won't carry us through the dark days of doubt and discouragement that family conflict brings. We need a more solid faith foundation for that.

Can we develop different eyes to see life's problems? Can we embrace them, even those that are painful and evil, and believe that God can redeem our pain and heartache? In his excellent book *Reaching for the Invisible God,* Philip Yancey recalls that Gregory of Nicea once called St. Basil's faith "ambidextrous." St. Basil welcomed both the good and the bad into his life because he was convinced that God would work good out of both. God not only allows pain in our experience; he uses it to mold us. In fact, God may allow the pain to crush us so he can form something new from the dust. Yancey quotes Jean-Pierre de Caussade who said, "A living faith is nothing else than a steadfast pursuit of God through all that disguises, disfigures, demolishes and seeks, so to speak, to abolish him." And he encouraged those who would listen: "Love and accept the present moment as the best, with perfect trust in God's universal goodness. . . . Everything without exception is an instrument and means of sanctification. . . . God's purpose for us is always what will contribute most to our good."[2]

We love to ask the *why* questions, and we demand that God pull back the curtain and give us a look into his deepest secrets of the universe. That rarely happens. Instead, it is more productive to accept the fact that we are fallen, though redeemed, people, and there are many things that will stay a mystery to us. In that humility, we look to God, trusting in his goodness and sovereignty, not demanding definitive answers.

The difference in our perception of God determines whether we see our struggles as a classroom or a prison. If our prayers are "Lord, please get me out of this!" then we see it as a prison. Instead, we can pray, "Lord, help me learn whatever lesson you want to teach. I'm listening, Father." We can't control God, and we can't control other people. All we can control is our response to each situation. We may not have had much practice, but we can learn to trust God even in the darkness, be honest even when a lie will fool somebody for a while, show kindness even when our hearts are breaking, and be strong even when we feel so weak.

It doesn't help to wish things were different. We can look back, but only for the purpose of seeing pain so that we can grieve and destructive behavior patterns so that we can repent. We need to be fully present where we are and to acknowledge the presence of God with us. A meaningful story in the Scriptures is the account of Paul and Silas in Philippi. These men were telling everyone everywhere about Christ. In fact, Christ had commissioned them to go to the entire world to spread the gospel. In Philippi, they led some people to salvation, and they cast out a demon from a slave girl. The girl's owners got a mob together, and they had Paul and Silas arrested. The magistrates ordered the two men to be stripped and beaten, then thrown into the deepest, darkest hole in the center of the prison. How would you respond in a situation like this? I know how I'd probably react. I'd say, "Hey, God, what's going on? I was serving you, doing what you wanted me to do, and look what happened. Get me out of this—now!"

But Paul and Silas didn't blame God. They trusted that God was still in control. Even in their beatings, even in the deepest pit of that prison, they still trusted God's goodness and sovereignty. Luke records: "About midnight Paul and Silas were praying and singing hymns to God, and the other prisoners were listening to them" (Acts 16:25). Instead of feeling sorry for themselves, they prayed. Instead of whining and blaming God, they sang hymns. Why did they pray and sing? I think it was because they knew that God was still in control. They weren't, but he was. Also, they trusted that God's purpose for them wasn't crushed by the beating and imprisonment. This was a classroom in which they were to learn, and they were good students. You and I need to pray, trusting God to use our pain for good, and you and I need to sing songs of joy because we are convinced that God is good and sovereign even in our deepest dungeon. If we're not convinced, maybe singing will help convince us.

God is a gracious and powerful redeemer. He is willing and able to use anything—failure, divorce, tragedy, addictions, abuse, abandonment, disease, death—and weave it into our lives for good, but there is one catch. We must trust him to do it. Our trust in his goodness and grace is the soil in which God's redemption grows. We don't need much trust, just enough to get started. As we are honest with God and seek his face, perhaps our trust will grow. A friend of mine wrestled with God about a strained and broken relationship. For years she prayed that God would change that person, but nothing happened. Finally, after many years of dashed hopes, my friend changed her prayer. She stopped praying that God would change that other person and started praying that God would change her. This is her prayer:

> Dear Father, you know my heart. My prayer today is for the gift of faith—to believe you are good and kind and strong and wise. I have hated the hurt in my heart, but now I want to accept it as an instrument to drive me to you. I have wandered in the desert. Now I want to live and learn there. Father, I think these years of hurt are a gift from you—a gift I never wanted but one I now realize I desperately needed. They are a gift to show me my great need for you. I thought I knew what was right before. I thought I knew what I wanted and needed. But I was wrong. I need your touch today. I need your peace and hope. I trust—maybe for the first time—that you are really God and you deserve my trust.

If you are reading this book, you are a conscientious parent who is committed to being the best mother or father you can be. I applaud that. But the best parent you can be starts not with behavior but with heart. I encourage you to look at the conflict you are having with your teenager (and your spouse and your parents and . . .) through a different set of lenses. Stop asking, "How can I get this resolved quickly?" and start asking, "Lord, what do you want to teach me through this? I'm listening, Father."

A Closer Look

1. Look at the green, yellow, and red lights in "Sometimes It's Them." Which one best describes your teenager? Explain.

2. Look at the green, yellow, and red lights in "Sometimes It's Us." Which one best describes you? Explain.

3. Make a list of the changes your family has experienced, both good and bad, throughout the past year. To help you think through those changes, look at the list on pages 60–61 and score a number for each stress, from 1 to 100. Add all these up. What does this number tell you about the stress you and your family have been experiencing?

4. How would it change you if you had "ambidextrous faith," accepting the good and the bad from God's hand?

FIVE

THE TRUTH AND NOTHING BUT THE TRUTH

When we think of conflict, we often visualize two people going head to head in heated confrontation. However, conflict has various ways of expressing itself. The challenge for all parents is to recognize the different temperaments and personality types of their children and realize that each child is going to respond to conflict in his or her own way. In this chapter we want to take a good, hard look at reality, not for the purpose of blame, but in order to see the truth so we can respond appropriately. We will look at patterns of behavior and thinking that result in different types of conflict in families.

Playing Roles

The more stress people feel, the more they are forced into particular roles that are designed to relieve their stress and help them gain a semblance of significance. These roles are an attempt to make sense of the world. Although they are effective to a degree, these roles prevent both the individual and the family from addressing the real problems that cause stress, worry, and heartache. Christian counselors and pastors have identified these roles in several different, helpful ways. For example, Dan Allender observed in his book *The Wounded Heart* that victims of sexual abuse often fall into the roles of Nice Girl (the one who tries to win acceptance by being sweet all the time), Party Girl (the one who tries to escape into drinking, sex, and wild living), and Tough Girl (the one who is determined to intimidate everybody and control everything so she will never be hurt again).[1] My list of stressed-related roles includes:

The hero. The hero is determined to be somebody by doing well—exceptionally well—in sports, academics, work, or some talent. Success makes him feel better about himself, and it takes some pressure off at home because the other family members can be proud of him instead of fighting.

The comic. When things get tense, the comic gets funny. This person cracks jokes and one-liners to lighten things up and relieve tension. She's laughing, but she's dying inside.

The mole. Some people try to get as far away from conflict as possible. They hide in their rooms, behind a newspaper, or in front of the television to avoid talking about real hurts. Hiding is meant to prevent hurting, but it also prevents resolution.

The general. Some of us respond to chaos by taking charge. If nobody else will tell people what to do, the general will!

The fixer. This person sees all the problems and is determined to solve them by making people feel better. The fixer often "reads" people's slightest changes in voice inflections or facial expressions so she can jump to do whatever it takes to make that person happy. She is seen as a wonderful servant, but her service is motivated by fear.

The nice guy or girl. This person lives in the midst of anger and strife but always smiles and has a kind word to say. This is an attempt to lower the level of tension, but it internalizes it instead of resolving it.

The scapegoat. In furious families, somebody has to get the blame. Too often, it is too threatening to say, "My father is an abusive alcoholic," or "My mother is a smothering, angry woman." Instead, we find someone easier to blame, someone who is less likely to fight back, and we pour all the anger, blame, and guilt on that poor soul.

The principle is this: the more a person feels insecure and unloved, the more he tries to play a role to find meaning in life. If the family is relatively stable and loving, role-playing may be almost nonexistent. If tension reigns, however, each person finds a role to play in the desperate attempt to make sense of life and reduce the stress around him. In such families, a certain pathological balance takes place: one attacks and one withdraws, one verbalizes and one internalizes, one is obsessed with fear about even the slightest thing and one is oblivious to even the most glaring problems. As I've counseled with scores of parents over the last several years, I've seen this "pattern of opposites." I've watched as one parent is hysterical or controlling or overprotective while the other is passive and uninvolved.

Getting Big, Getting Little

One Christian counselor observed that in conflict, some people "get little" and some people "get big."[2] Some of us wither under stress. Our voices get softer, our posture becomes submissive, we stammer and avoid any definitive statements. Our response is to become so small that we vanish! On the other hand, some of us get loud, demanding, and coarse. We bristle with anger and demand that others comply. We take charge and defy anyone to get in our way. We try to be huge and tower over everybody else. Ironically, these two very different people are often married to each other!

If parents' conflict with a teenager is prolonged, even a stable home can become full of tension and uncertainty. Each person gradually begins to play a role in an attempt to cope. Quite often, the other children, the "good kids," feel neglected as the parents focus their attention on the open wound of the teenager who is out of control. The forgotten child may gravitate to one of these unhealthy roles first and become the "canary in the mine" by being the first indication of serious family upheaval. Even so, that canary may not cry out for attention. Instead, it may "get little" and hide in the corner, hoping nobody yells or blames or hurts it again. I've known some parents who were so stressed about a defiant, out-of-control child that they were only too glad for their other child to become passive and not demand any attention at all. Parents must pay attention to the other children and determine how they are faring. They may be hurting just as much as the one who is screaming for attention.

Of course, roles can be played by each member of the family, not just the children. Parents often bring their roles into the marriage from the unresolved stresses of their own childhoods. Added stresses of the new family can harden these roles unless the person is brave enough to see the truth and repent.

Wrong Goals

Another common problem is that parents have wrong and distorted goals in life. The Scriptures state clearly that the focus of our desires should be to love God with all our hearts (see Matt. 22:36–39). Paul said it this way: "What is more, I consider everything a loss compared to the surpassing greatness of knowing Christ Jesus my Lord, for whose sake I have lost all things. I consider them rubbish, that I may gain Christ" (Phil. 3:8–9).

If we were honest (and that's what this book and this chapter are about), many of us would have to admit that we desire success, pleasure, and approval far more than the purpose and presence of Christ in our lives. We think far more about how to achieve a promotion or get more money or win an important friend than about hearing "Well done, good and faithful servant" from God. Whether we like it or not, we are models for our children. They hear our conversations, and they see what makes us excited or discouraged. If we value things and status more than God and people, our children absorb those perspectives. I've talked to kids who come from very successful and socially powerful homes, but what I hear is that some of them feel that they are either a hindrance or a trophy to their parents. They either get in the way of their parents' goals, or they are something their parents can point to and say, "Look what I've done." That's not love.

CHOICES

Each of us is responsible before God for our choices. I've known courageous teenagers from rotten homes who made the choice to be honest and follow a path of integrity, unlike anything they knew as children. Conversely, I've known young people from stable, loving homes who took step after step into deception and sin. They certainly knew better, and they had all the support and encouragement a person could want. Still, they chose to take one small step on the wrong path, and that step took them down a long, slippery slope of pain and heartache.

Rachel was a person like that. I met her when she was a little girl when I spoke at a church in Missouri many years ago. Her parents were (and are) fine, loving people. Rachel was a sweet, sensitive girl, and very bright. She was an only child, and she excelled at almost everything she tried. In junior high school she was in the band and on the volleyball team. She had lots of friends. After the eighth grade, her father was promoted in his engineering firm and was transferred from Kansas City to St. Louis. They were all excited but, of course, a bit anxious about the move. Within a few weeks, they had found a new church and were making friends. Rachel was a hit in the new youth group! The girls invited her to spend the night or go to the mall or the movies, and for the first time boys began to show interest in her.

When the first few boys called, Rachel was very shy. She talked for a while, but when she ran out of things to say, she simply said, "Gotta go" and hung up. Gradually, one boy's calls became more regular. Soon he and Rachel were talking every night. Will was a quiet boy. Rachel's parents thought he was OK at best but not the kind of young man they envisioned for their daughter. But of course, there was plenty of time for new boyfriends down the road.

During her freshman year Will and Rachel became inseparable. Gradually, the circle of friends narrowed. At first, Rachel's parents hardly noticed. She still went out with Will in a group, but now the friends were Will's, not hers. Rachel's sweet disposition changed too. She became withdrawn and defensive, not the sweet, gentle girl her parents had known. They became concerned enough to talk to their pastor and some trusted friends, but everyone assured them, "Oh, it's normal for a girl her age. Don't worry about it." So they didn't.

By the middle of her sophomore year, Will and Rachel were together as much as possible. Will, now a senior, picked her up in the morning and brought her home after school . . . or late at night if they had something else to do. Rachel's parents tried to steer her toward a wider group of friends, but Rachel often reacted, "What's the matter? Don't you like Will? Don't you think I can pick my own friends?" And then in a huff, "I'm not a little child anymore!" Her parents pleaded and threatened. They set curfews and requirements. Sometimes Rachel cooperated for a while, but she always went back to Will at school and found excuses to spend time with him. He was at every youth group event so he could be with her. The parents thought about changing churches, but they knew he'd just follow them. They thought about forbidding their daughter to go to the youth group, but that seemed ludicrous.

Rachel's identity was wrapped up in this intense, quiet boy. Something about him was attractive to her, but it was more than attraction. She was absorbed in him. She gradually lost her ability to think for herself. She became an extension of Will—nothing more, nothing less. She thought his thoughts, wanted his desires, went where he went, and dreamed his dreams.

In the spring of that year, something happened between them (Was Will looking at another girl?), and Will and Rachel broke up. It was a traumatic mess for Rachel. She raged and wept for a week and then became depressed. Her parents felt compassion for her, but they were thrilled to get Will out of her life. Now, they thought, she would get some breathing room and go back to being her old self again.

The old Rachel did return—for about a month. She was sweet, considerate, and thoughtful. In fact, in a moment of self-revelation, she told her mother, "I don't know how you put up with me the last year!" Her mother replied, "I don't know how I did either." They hugged each other and laughed.

Another boy soon had his eyes on Rachel. Like a hawk swooping down on an unwary rabbit, he got her in his sights and clamped his talons on her heart. Richard was a tall, handsome young man, a loner as intense as Will. This time Rachel's dad was wise and on guard. After Richard had called her a couple of times and Rachel had expressed delight when he called, her father asked Rachel to bring him to the house so he could meet him.

When Richard walked in the door, Rachel's dad recognized the same look in his eye that Will had had—the determination to conquer someone. After a few minutes of small talk, her dad dropped a bomb. He looked squarely at the young man and said, "Richard, we don't know you well, and you don't really know us, but there's one thing I want you to understand. My daughter is very precious to me, and you'd better not hurt her."

Rachel and her mother gasped. Rachel was flabbergasted and embarrassed. "Dad, how could you say such a thing? Richard is a guest in our home . . . and you invited him here!" Richard knew exactly what Rachel's dad was saying. He just smiled and nodded in a knowing way. To him, the conquest was now going to be just a bit more challenging. He liked that.

Rachel's dad responded, "If you treat her with respect and honor, we will get along just fine. If not . . ." He didn't need to finish his sentence. Everyone in the room knew exactly what he meant.

Sadly, the warning had as much effect as spitting in the wind. In a short time, Rachel was just as absorbed in Richard as she had been in Will—maybe more. In fact, the look in her eyes told her parents that this was a serious problem. She stayed out late almost every night talking to Richard in the car in the driveway. Sometimes her mother or father went out to get her to come in. Sometimes they met her at the door. When they challenged her about doing what Richard wanted her to do every waking moment, she sometimes shrugged and walked away, but in a few telling moments, she exploded, "You don't understand. I have to do what he wants!" Her parents tried to counsel her: "You can make your own decisions. You don't have to do what he demands. Be yourself." Their admonitions fell on deaf ears.

Rachel's parents tried everything they could try. They prayed, and they called friends to pray. They claimed passages of Scripture, and they talked to their pastor. They went to a counselor to get help. They read stacks of books and cried a flood of tears. They threatened consequences and promised rewards. They tried to follow through on both, but the consequences only drove Rachel further into Richard's arms, and the promises couldn't compare to Richard's promise of intimacy and belonging. Rachel and her parents had long arguments and short outbursts. The warmth and laughter they had enjoyed as a family a few short years ago now seemed like a distant memory. Where did that sweet little girl go?

During her senior year, Rachel's relationship with Richard became so intense that even Rachel wanted out. She tried to talk to him to get him to agree that this was the best course, but when he shook his head, she felt stuck. She was so wrapped up in pleasing him in every way, she felt she needed his approval to break away—approval he would never give. He had exactly what he wanted—a slave.

Once Rachel turned eighteen, her parents' demands carried less weight. They threatened to kick her out of the house if she continued to see Richard, but they knew she would go to live with him. They suspected that the two were doing more than just talking late at night, and they confronted her to find out the truth. She denied any sexual activity, and she told them she deeply resented them not having confidence in her. Her mother pleaded, "Just give us a reason to have confidence in you, honey. We want more than anything to trust you, but look at how much you are under his thumb. You don't make any of your own decisions. It's like his voice is in your head telling you what to do all the time." Rachel stomped out of the house and found Richard to console her.

One day, Rachel's dad came home after work and found his wife and daughter sitting on the sofa crying. "What's wrong?" he asked, but they both just cried. "Is somebody hurt?" he insisted. "Tell me what's going on."

Rachel couldn't talk, but after a moment her mother quietly looked up and said through tear-filled eyes, "Rachel's pregnant."

Her dad's head spun with the implications of that statement. Marriage. A bum for a son-in-law. Or adoption. Or the trials of being a single mother and unwanted by good, Christian young men. The images pounded his mind as the truth sank in.

After a few minutes, Rachel's mother turned to her daughter and said through her sobs, "Well, I guess you two should just get married."

Her father exploded, "No! Don't make a bad thing that much worse. There are lots better choices than being married to somebody like Richard." He stumbled for words. "It would be better to raise the child yourself or put it up for adoption. Or we could raise it." Then depression hit him. He sat heavily on the sofa and wept too. It was the only appropriate response.

What happened? How did it come to this? How did a sweet, compliant, gentle girl become the target of two oppressive young wolves? Why couldn't her loving, supportive parents get through to her? People make choices, and those choices have serious consequences. In this case, a gentle girl was susceptible to the wiles of a controlling boy. One thing led to another, and her capacity to make her own decisions was compromised until she was unable to see reality and break away. It was a classic case of "frog in the kettle"—Rachel found herself in hot water because the temperature was raised so gradually she never even noticed.

Rachel's unexpected and unplanned pregnancy forced Rachel to look at herself, her boyfriend, her family, and future in a whole new way. Like many young men who are determined to conquer their quest, they become cowards when faced with the real consequences of wrong behavior. Richard eventually begins to fade from Rachel and her family once the reality of his responsibilities became more evident. Richard's family didn't encourage his commitment and responsibility to Rachel either.

Eventually, the choice to keep the baby and take on the responsibility of motherhood was the only good and right decision for Rachel to make. Through her unfortunate circumstances, Rachel and her family drew close together and formed a new bond of love between them unlike anything they had ever experienced. In spite of how bad a situation might seem, Romans 8:28 teaches "And we know that in all things God works for the good of those who love him, who have been called according to his purpose" (NIV).

In Rachel's case, Bad became Good because it caused her to grow and see life differently. She learned to face her future with maturity knowing the importance of making right choices. As parents, we must not only model good decisions but encourage them and affirm them when they make right choices.

Remember, no matter how difficult and hopeless a situation might seem in the eyes of our teenagers, we must teach them how to avoid wrong decisions when tempted with Satan's lies. Young people need to know that God has already made a way of escape for them if they are willing to take it.

Where Is God?

Christian parents sometimes look at the chaos in their families and wonder, "Where is God in this? Doesn't he care?" Disappointment is a natural and normal response, even disappointment with God. Many of us want our faith and our lives to be neat, clean, and orderly. We expect God to do certain things because we've prayed or because we've done the right thing, but life is much more complex than simple cause-effect. We are all fallen people living in a fallen world, and people make their own choices—sometimes very bad choices—even though we've prayed and trusted God on their behalf.

If you feel resentful toward God, take some time to read the Book of Job. This righteous man suffered as much as any man. Though we talk about the "patience of Job" as if he quietly waited for God's solution, the Scriptures show him angry, despairing, and arguing with his friends and with God. Things weren't working out the way he planned or expected, and he was ticked off! His situation left him confused, hurt, and alone. When God appears at the end of the book, he doesn't rebuke Job for asking hard questions, though God does rebuke the friends who offered Job only simple and condemning answers. God's message to Job is not directly about his suffering. In fact, God doesn't even mention any of Job's pains and problems. God reminds him that he is the sovereign Lord of the universe. He is wise, kind, and powerful. Even when we don't understand what is going on, God is still trustworthy. He accomplishes his purposes even when we can't see them.

It is far better to argue and plead with God than to give up on him and walk away. God doesn't condemn us for being confused, so ask all the hard questions you need to ask. Eventually, you will be reminded that God is near and he is good. You can trust him.

A Closer Look

I want to conclude this chapter with some questions and suggestions for determining the truth in your family struggles. Remember, the goal is not to blame anyone. The goal is to uncover truth so each person can respond appropriately. You may find that you are causing much of the problem by modeling your own unresolved hurts and anger, or you may find that your child has made some tragic decisions that have taken him down a long, destructive path. In most cases, responsibility rests on both sides. Have the courage to admit your own culpability in the cause or in your angry or passive response to your child's behavior.

1. You have already described the stress your family has experienced in the past few years. Now take that insight a step further. What roles do you see each person in the family playing? List each person, and see how they match the roles described in this chapter.

2. In what way is your family environment contributing to the problem?
   - Is there comparison between the "good kid" and the "bad kid"? How is that comparison communicated?
   - Are children a nuisance or a trophy to you or your spouse?
   - How is anger resolved between you and your spouse or between you and your ex?
   - Has there been a significant stressor in the recent past, such as a divorce, death, disease, or a move? If so, how did you prepare your children to handle it?

3. Reflect on the wrong goals described in this chapter (success, pleasure, and approval instead of loving and serving Christ). To what degree have these been true of your heart's desire? How much time do you spend thinking and daydreaming about each one?

4. How would your teenager answer this question: What is the root cause of tension and conflict in our family?

5. How would your spouse or ex answer the question: What is the root cause of tension and conflict in our family?

6. How would you answer the question: What is the root cause of tension and conflict in our family?

7. If you are unsure of what is going on in your teenager's life, how can you find out?
    - What demeanor do you observe?
    - What significant changes have taken place in his or her behavior?
    - Are there other parents you can ask to tell you what they observe about your teenager?
    - Is there a school counselor or youth pastor you can ask for observations?

SIX

GET A H.A.N.D.L.E. ON RESOLVING CONFLICT

I've watched many parents as they attempted to resolve conflict with their teenagers. Some have done it well, but many, who sincerely wanted to take steps to rebuild trust and open lines of communication, have driven more wedges between themselves and their kids. Some have been too protective and failed to let their young adults take responsibility for their actions. Some have been too passive and failed to clarify their expectations and enforce consequences. Some have "gotten big" and squashed meaningful interaction, and some have "gotten little" and walked away or been intimidated. Some have used rage instead of reason, and some have simply given up. I want to offer a strategy that has been helpful to many parents, a strategy that gives you a H.A.N.D.L.E. on resolving conflict.[1]

PREPARATION

Before we get to the principles of the actual interaction, it is vitally important for us to get prepared. The old Boy Scout motto—

Be prepared—is appropriate in many settings, and this is one of them. Be a student of the past. How have you and your teenager handled conflict over the past few years and months? In most cases, a clear pattern is evident even with casual observation. If you have yelled and demanded compliance in the past, it is likely that you will be tempted to do that in the future. If your spouse has taken the side of your teenager in past conflict, that is likely next time too. If your teenager has stomped out, yelled, or sulked away in the last few times you have struggled together, expect the same thing again. You might think of the roles we examined in the last chapter. These can help you recognize the patterns of how people respond to stress in conflict. Observing the past allows you to anticipate the future, and that is a terrific help when getting ready for difficult conversations.

One of the biggest decisions for many of us is to determine to have the conversation at all. We may think, *He won't do it again. Surely he's wised up by now. If I just let it go, it will go away, and everything will be all right.* Wrong! Time doesn't heal all wounds, and denial doesn't fix problems. If tension has become the norm in a relationship, it's time to take action. That action, however, needs to be guided by reason, objectivity, and wisdom, not rage and fear.

I've known many parents who feared they would go "brain dead" when they finally sat down with their teenager to talk about the real, tough issues in their lives. In conflict, these parents have the habit of becoming invisible, not just little! My advice to them is to write out exactly what they want to say on a piece of paper and put it in their pocket. Then, if they become mush-brained, they can say, "I want to be sure I say what I really want to say. Let me read this to you." Then they can read what they have written on the paper. Does this make them less effective? No, not at all. It makes them far more effective than they would be if they failed to speak their minds. If you need to do this, go for it!

Try to pick a time that has the most promise for success, but be realistic. There is probably no time when your teenager will enjoy a conversation like this! Although it is sometimes wise to have the discussion at the point of conflict, in most cases, it is best to let the passions cool a bit before you discuss the situation. Of course, it does little good to try to reason with someone who is high on alcohol or drugs. If a teenager comes in later than her curfew, you might say, "We need to talk about this in the morning." That way, you have set the time and the agenda. No one is surprised.

Pick a place that is most conducive to reason and good communication. Don't try to have this conversation in front of your teenager's little brother. Make sure you choose a comfortable space and allow sufficient time to talk things out. If your teenager (or spouse) wants to leave, ask him to stay. If he insists on leaving, you can affirm that the reason you want to talk is that you love him very much and you want to build trust. Also, confirm that you aren't going to quit. You will keep pursuing, with reason and kindness, as long as it takes.

Many parents have let things go unresolved for so long that the first conversation is like the cap blowing off Mount St. Helens! Don't be surprised at volcanic emotions and wild accusations. Later, as communication is better, you will be able to talk things out more quickly and more reasonably without letting them build to the boiling point.

Getting a H.A.N.D.L.E.

Now let's look at the principles of resolving conflict.

H—*Hang in there! Stay cool!*

>Solomon said:
>>A fool gives full vent to his anger,
>>but a wise man keeps himself under control.
>>>(Prov. 29:11)

If you have prepared well and you anticipate your own response and the reaction of your teenager, you will be ready for any manipulation she throws at you. If she has used self-pity in the past, she will probably use it here. If she has blamed you and your divorce in the past, she'll use the same blame and excuses again. Be ready so you can stay in control of your emotions.

Some teenagers have won a lot of confrontations with their parents by getting them into arguments. They blame, they condemn, they point fingers. If they can get you into an argument, they feel they have won. Stay out of the arguments. You are the adult; act like one. I recommend that you use a very simple but powerful formula of "I messages" in these conversations: "I feel," "I want," "I will."

When Tim took his father's car without asking permission (again), his dad decided it was time to do something about it instead of ignoring the problem. He told Tim he wanted to talk with him. They sat down in the living room, away from Tim's younger brother and sister. Soon after his dad began, Tim gave lots of excuses, such as, "But I needed the car, and you weren't here. You're *never* here when I need you."

In the past, Tim's dad got caught up in defending himself for his work schedule and travel for his company. No, he certainly wasn't there every minute of every day, and Tim often used that as leverage to blame his dad for his own bad decisions. This time, Tim's dad didn't take the bait. Instead, he responded using "I messages": "Son, *I feel* hurt when you take things of mine without asking. *I want* to have a terrific relationship with you, but there's a problem. *I want* you to ask me before you take the car. Every time. No exceptions. If you take it again without asking, *I will* withhold it from you for two weeks. Is that clear to you?"

If the conversation gets too hot, call a time-out so tempers can cool and reason can prevail. Be sure to set a time to get back together, preferably in a few minutes. You might say, "This is getting a little too intense right now. Let's take a break for ten minutes and come back. Maybe then we can find a reasonable solution."

A—Admit Your Anger

No matter how much we try to hide our anger, our teenager knows very well that we are ticked off. Perhaps it's the smoke coming out of our ears that gives it away! Instead of saying, "I'm not really mad at you. I just want the best for you," be honest; state the truth by saying, "I feel angry when you don't follow through with the commitments you have made." This honesty is especially recommended for those parents who are afraid of speaking the truth. Be careful, however, if you are a person who becomes volatile in tense situations; don't let this be a springboard for an angry outburst. Instead, talk about the emotion that is often underneath the anger: *hurt*. You could say, "It hurts me when you walk away without resolving things. I want us to have a trusting relationship."

After admitting your anger, move quickly to state your goal for the conversation. After all, your purpose is not just to vent your emotions. You want to find common ground, to understand, to clear away miscommunication and find a workable solution to rebuild trust. If you say these things, your teenager will know this conversation is not designed just to blast; it is meant to build. That can make a tremendous difference in the direction and outcome of the talk.

N—No Judgment Allowed

We've already talked about using "I messages" like "I feel," "I want," and "I will." Most of us have used "you messages" that are meant to blame and condemn. Whether we point our fingers or not, the message we give is not subtle: "You have messed up again, and you better straighten up right now!" That kind of message makes a person defensive. It produces a fight-or-flight reaction, and neither of those reactions helps resolve the problem. Instead of saying, "You keep going out and getting drunk," you could say, "I'm worried about you. When you drink, I'm afraid for your safety and your health."

Another common mistake is using words like *always* and *never:* "You *never* listen when I'm talking to you." These words paint a bleak picture of the person and communicate hopelessness and condemnation. It would be much better to change the statement to: "I feel hurt when I try to communicate with you and you shut me out."

Focus on the behavior of the person, not the person himself. If your daughter is spending her time with the wrong crowd, don't say, "You are so stupid!" Instead, you can say, "I love you so much, and I'm concerned that you are picking up habits from your new friends that are harmful to you. I want us to talk about that."

Learning to use "I messages" and avoiding judgment is a learned skill. Practice it as preparation for the conversation, perhaps in less-heated meetings with people at work, in the neighborhood, at church, and at home. Soon this skill can become second nature, and you'll be disarming people instead of condemning them.

Look for every opportunity to affirm your teenager, even (and especially) in the middle of a tense conversation. From time to time, I've asked troubled parents to tell me something positive about their teenager. Quite often the parents stumble for a minute or two and can't think of anything to say. They have become so consumed with the teenager's problems that they've lost sight of any strengths and talents. In your preparation, think of things you appreciate about your son or daughter. Make sure you bring those up early and appropriately often in the conversation. This will help you appear to be a cheerleader instead of a prison warden. It makes a difference!

It is possible to turn even the biggest difficulties into positives. One man's son was as defiant as any fourteen-year-old could be. No matter what his father asked him to do, the son refused. The dad gave him consequences, but the boy endured them without breaking. This went on for months, until one day, God gave this dad a vision. He saw how God might someday turn the tenacity in his son's defiance into a great strength. If this boy could be so stubborn about saying no to his father, someday he might channel this same tenacity toward doing great things for God. This perspective gave the father a new sense of hope, and he communicated his hope to his son (who thought his father had gone nuts, but that's OK). In many cases, our biggest weaknesses are strengths gone awry—tenacity becomes defiance, creativity becomes irresponsibility, and sensitivity becomes the need to win approval. Take a step back and look at how the thing you despise in your teenager today might someday be your child's greatest strength if God turns that weakness back into a strength. Patience and persistence are great virtues in raising teenagers. Solomon wrote:

> Better a patient man than a warrior,
> a man who controls his temper than one who
> takes a city. (Prov. 16:32)

D—Deal with the Facts

All too often, I've seen parents bring up things they suspect with their teenagers and lose the argument because they don't have proof. Deal with the facts, not conjecture. If your child is late, you may suspect she has been involved in vandalism or sexual activity, but unless you can prove it, stick with the clear, identifiable truth of her being late. Address that fact clearly. You may want to bring up your suspicions, but only after you have addressed the known violations with enforceable consequences.

Some parents store up a backlog of offenses and then pounce on their kids with 376 things they've done wrong. Using a dump truck method is not effective . . . except to condemn the person dumped on. Stick with one or maybe two problems, and give specific examples of the offenses. There should be little or no room for the teenager to disagree with the facts. Oh sure, he'll have a dozen excuses for every one of them, but your point is that the behavior is unacceptable, and it must change.

Work toward a real solution. If possible, involve your teenager in the process by asking, "What do you think is the right thing to do here?" You might be surprised to find that your teenager suggests a harsher set of consequences than you envisioned. Maybe not. Try to work out a compromise or a staggered implementation based on credible performance. For example, if your daughter's grades are bad, you might tell her she can have certain privileges with the car if she passes every course, more if she averages a B, and more if she makes an A or two. Spell this out clearly. In fact, it is wise to put this agreement in writing so there is no misunderstanding a few weeks later when the report cards come out.

Compromises aren't appropriate in some cases. Drugs, sex, raves, and other dangerous activities do not allow bargaining. They are destructive, sinful, and wrong. Draw the line where you feel God wants it to be. Don't get into shouting matches about these things. State the boundaries and the consequences clearly, and stick to them.

If the facts become muddled or if conflict persists for a while, I suggest you find a third party to give you wise counsel. Find someone who isn't involved in the problem so he has no vested interest in taking sides. Your pastor, a parent who has experience with a troubled teenager of her own, or a Christian counselor can bring light and hope to a dismal situation.

L—Listen

In the heat of confrontation, the last thing many of us want to do is listen. If our goal is to blast, that's completely valid, but if our goal is to build, we need to learn to listen carefully to the other person. One of the best ways to understand someone is to ask questions. Take a deep breath, calm down, and say, "Would you tell me more of what you're thinking about that? I want to understand your perspective." After the smelling salts have worn off, that person will probably be much more likely to enter into genuine give-and-take instead of blast and scrape. Even when you think you understand the person's reasoning, ask questions anyway to be sure you get the picture.

Another way to be sure you understand (and to be sure the person has said what he thinks he's said) is to reflect back what the person is saying to you. Say, "This is what I think you're telling me...." Sometimes the person will respond, "Yes, you've got it," but sometimes we have missed them completely, and they respond, "No, you still don't understand." Ask them to explain again, and don't quit until you understand. Now, be careful; the purpose here is so that you understand, not that you agree. Those are often two different things in a heated or tense conversation.

If we want the person to feel understood, we may want to affirm the emotions we see in them. If your son is gritting his teeth and refuses to look at you, you might say, "Son, you're angry." Or if your daughter is crying, you might want to say, "Honey, I know you're afraid." Don't phrase these as questions to be answered. Let them stand as observations that communicate understanding, and let them go at that. This is a wonderful way to draw people out and stimulate real, rich discussions. If your teenager is out of control, however, don't use this method. Affirming rage only engenders more rage, and that's not productive or helpful.

Many of us think we are listening when we are quiet, but sometimes we are using that time to think of the next time we get to talk. That's not listening; it's sermon preparation! When your teenager is talking, be fully present. Give your undivided attention and absorb the words, the inflections, and the nonverbal communication.

James wrote the believers of his day: "My dear brothers, take note of this: Everyone should be quick to listen, slow to speak and slow to become angry, for man's anger does not bring about the righteous life that God desires" (James 1:19–20). His encouragement is just as necessary today as it was two millennia ago.

E—Evaluate

During the discussion, be aware of yourself and how you are handling the situation. A friend of mine told me that when he was having a tense conversation with his son, he found himself sliding down in his chair and letting his voice taper off into a whisper. He thought, *Hey, I'm "getting little." I can do better than that!* He sat up straight and became himself again in the discussion. He became more assertive and engaged, and he said the things he had long needed to say. Self-awareness made a huge difference in this instance and in their relationship from that day on.

After the conversation, reflect on what happened, and learn from it. Many of us drift toward assigning blame after a big discussion like this. We viciously blame our teenager or spouse or ourselves for saying something stupid or for not saying enough. For many of us, just engaging our teenager is a major step forward, and we need to be gracious with ourselves if we have had the courage to fight through our fears and speak the truth, however faltering that truth may have come out of our mouths. Others of us may realize that we needed to listen more or that we became too agitated. We may not have done it perfectly, but we did it, and that's a big step forward. Next time we can prepare a bit better and handle ourselves better.

Make sure you don't judge yourself according to the response of your teenager. You may have done it perfectly, but your son or daughter may have chosen to blow you off. After all, the Lord Jesus himself spoke truth more clearly than anyone ever did, and look what they did to him.

Now What?

The hours and days after a major confrontation can be the hardest of our lives. We may feel guilty or furious—or both at the same time. If you struggle with making sense of things, talk to a trusted friend or pastor or counselor to get some perspective.

If your teenager responds well to the discussion, it is a step—but only a step—toward genuine trust. Many more need to be taken. Trust is built as patterns of responsibility and respect are demonstrated over time. One good response is a step forward, but don't assume everything is over. Years of silence or blaming can't be overcome in one conversation. Healing takes time and attention.

Let the next conversation be as positive as possible. Keep looking for things to affirm in your teenager, even if she doesn't respond in kind. Sooner or later your words of kindness and grace will take hold.

Some parents expect and demand instant repentance when they lay down the law. A more reasonable path, especially for families that have bottled up their pain for years, is to ask your teenager to think about what you've said and talk again in a day or so. This defuses the passion of the moment and allows time for reason and reflection. If your teenager still is defiant, be clear about the consequences. Your commitment to be loving and firm (yes, they can go together) is the fertile ground of real change—for your teenager and for you.

If there is no sign of change over weeks and months, get help. Ask a trained professional to meet with you, your spouse, and your teenager to give you the help you need to begin to rebuild trust in the relationships. Sometimes the web of deceit, confusion, and bitterness is simply too great for us to untangle on our own, and we need someone to give us insight and skills to take the steps we so desperately want to take.

Learning the Skill

The principles and examples in this chapter are designed for parents who anticipate tense, full-blown confrontation with their teenagers. These principles, however, are useful for a broad range of interactions, from mild and commonplace to intense. As you grasp these insights and learn these skills, you will be able to use them in any and every situation with your teenager so the tension is diffused more quickly and doesn't build to the boiling point. You can also use these skills in other relationships in your life.

Speaking of other relationships. . . . Now that we've covered these steps for handling and resolving conflict, you may realize that the most important element of preparation is for you and your spouse (or you and your ex) to come to agreement on the process before you actually talk to your teenager. If you try to resolve conflict with your teenager before establishing a mutual agreement with your spouse, the discussion may cause more confusion and take your family backward instead of forward. I've often seen one parent try to resolve things while the other defends the defiant teenager. This kind of triangle leaves one side defiant and triumphant while the other side becomes discouraged and furious. Take the time necessary to find common ground with your spouse. Agree on the main principles even if you agree to disagree on others. If you simply can't agree on a reasonable, workable process, seek the help of a pastor or Christian counselor. This inability of parents to agree on the basics of conflict resolution and purpose in their family is a huge red flag indicating needs in the entire family system.

No matter what, don't give up. I've seen God work miracles in families where there seemed to be no hope left at all. Those miracles were shouldered on the backs of courageous parents who kept looking to God and finding a way in the darkness. I have the utmost respect for these parents, who often found that a share of the problem was in themselves. They were willing to admit their sin and seek real change in order to show love to their precious teenagers.

A Closer Look

1. What do you need to do to be prepared for a confrontation with your teenager? What are the patterns in the past that help you anticipate future responses?

2. H—Hang in There! Stay Cool!: What do you need to do to stay in control and not get big or little?

3. A—Admit Your Anger: How would admitting your anger defuse the situation?

4. N—No Judgment Allowed: Describe some differences in the impact of "I messages" and "you messages." How do words like *always* and *never* make you feel when others use them on you?

5. D—Deal with the Facts: How do people respond when we accuse them using suspicions and theories instead of facts?

6. L—Listen: Read the section on listening again. Which of the principles do you need to apply most? Explain.

7. E—Evaluate: How would you rate yourself on a scale of 1–10 (1 being bad, 10 being good) in confrontation? Do you tend to blame yourself or others when things don't go well?

8. What would a genuine trusting relationship with your teenager look like?

SEVEN

CONSTRUCTIVE CONSEQUENCES

In the last chapter, we looked at principles of confrontation to resolve conflict. I mentioned that it is important to give your teenagers clear consequences for their behavior. Many parents are confused about the purpose and the process of administering consequences. I hope this chapter answers a lot of those questions.

Empty threats don't work. Pleading only shows your weakness and harms the relationship. Ignoring the problem doesn't solve anything. I've known scores of parents who know only these three methods of dealing with their children's depression or defiance. When I talk about constructive consequences, these parents look at me like I'm talking about differential calculus or quantum mechanics (unless, of course, they are mathematicians or physicists).

LOVE IS . . .

Many of us need to take a good, hard look at how we define *love*. We may think that love is making someone happy; therefore, if they aren't happy—and especially if they aren't happy with us—then we aren't loving them. Similarly, if someone has a problem, we think that love means we have to fix it for them. Love, though, is acting toward someone with their best interests at heart. When we take a child to get an immunization, the needle hurts for a moment, but most of us would agree that this act is in the child's best interest. As children grow up, however, our understanding of what's in their best interest gets fuzzier. Our own needs for love and security get caught up in their joys and struggles, and we sometimes forget how to be parents of young adults. We got joy out of fixing the hurts of our kids when they were young, so we errantly believe that they (and we) will feel better if we continue to fix them, even when they are in high school (for some parents, even when they are fifty years old).

- It isn't love to keep bailing someone out so he doesn't have to suffer from his bad choices.
- It isn't love to plead and threaten without giving clear consequences.
- It isn't love to ignore a problem and hope it will go away.
- It isn't love to treat a young adult like a child.

The most loving thing you can do for an irresponsible person is to let him face the consequences of his behavior. Remember, the goal of parenting is to produce mature, independent, responsible adults. If we bail children out too often, we block that goal. In fact, the effects of unfulfilled threats are many and severe.

- The young person learns the parent can't be trusted to follow through.
- She believes her parents really don't care.
- He believes consequences are a pipe dream, and he can do whatever he wants with impunity.
- She learns that emotional outbursts are the main way to communicate.

- He becomes a poor model to his own children, and the pathology is passed along to another generation.

Their Reaction?

When we impose consequences on our teenagers, how can we expect them to respond? Here's a clue: They aren't going to thank us! No, far more often I've seen them blame us: "You're so unfair! How could you do this to me?" Other times they use self-pity and pitiful pleas: "Please don't do this. I'll never do it again. I've never had a chance to do well. Just give me one more chance." Some even react with outbursts of rage complete with expletives, yelling, and stomping out of the room. Teens typically use whatever means they have used in the past to manipulate their parents—now they simply do it more intensely.

As you read and think and pray about the kind of consequences you need to set for your teenager, realize that the early stages are often a war for control. There will be a critical time when you are tempted to give in again and back down from this path. At that moment, you have a choice: to stand strong in the face of tremendous manipulation and feelings of internal guilt or to show weakness. Years ago, Dr. James Dobson wrote a wonderful book titled *Love Must Be Tough*. His message was true then, and it is just as true today. If we love our teenagers, sometimes we have to be tough enough to do what's right.

Setting consequences for your teenager may cause you to see in a new way the hurts in your own life. Your fears of disappointing your teenager by not fixing her problem may reveal a deep wound that has never been healed. See this as a gift from God. Although it is not the kind of gift you look forward to, it can meet your deepest need for hope and healing. Every struggle can be seen from God's perspective as an opportunity to learn and grow. This situation is no different. As you think about consequences for your teenager, be aware of what God is doing in your own heart. Healing there may be the first miracle God wants to work in your family.

CONTROL OR CHOICES

Early in this book we looked at the stages of development from child into adulthood. When our children are very young, our responsibility is to control their environment to protect them and provide for them. As they grow, however, our job as parents changes. As we consider the ultimate goal of producing responsible adults, we gradually give them more choices. Some of their decisions are simple, like what they want at McDonald's. As they get into adolescence, however, these decisions take on more significance. Our teens determine which classes they want to take, which sports to play or clubs to join, which friends to choose, and what forms of entertainment they want to enjoy. They experiment with almost every aspect of life, and we hope their experimentation doesn't lead them out of bounds. Of course we are there to guide and counsel, but we hope they will make virtually all their own decisions by the time they reach eighteen and leave home. That's the theory, anyway.

When our teenagers make dumb decisions, we sometimes feel compelled to step in and correct them. And when they make the same dumb decisions over and over again, we move back into the mode of parenting a little child. We feel compelled to control their behavior again. This, I believe, is a mistake in our reasoning, judgment, and actions. We need to continue to treat them like young adults. That means we give them choices, and we don't try to control their behavior by fixing, threatening, or pleading.

GUIDELINES FOR CONSEQUENCES

The choices we give our teenagers need to be:
Clear. We need to communicate what we expect their behavior to

be and what the rewards and punishments will be if they fail to comply. This needs to be communicated before the punishment is applied.

Attainable. Tailor the requirements so the teenager can meet them. If they are too difficult, we cause more tension with accusations; if they are too easy, we fail to accomplish our goal of developing responsibility.

Consistent. I've talked to some teenagers who said they had to guess what their parents wanted from them from day to day. That's not helpful, and it destroys trust. Don't change the requirements without talking about it first with your teenager and your spouse too.

Agreed upon. Each person needs to understand clearly the requirements and the outcome of compliance or noncompliance. Your teenager doesn't have to like it, but he needs to agree to abide by it. Some parents use a written contract that the teenager and the parents sign. I've seen this be very helpful in many cases where there has been a lot of misunderstanding.

Expandable. In some cases the requirements can be changed if the teenager meets certain criteria. For example, if he makes certain grades, he may receive particular privileges with the car, and if he makes higher grades, he can have the car for more time.

Enforceable. A consequence is no good at all if it is not enforceable. For that reason, attitudes are usually not the kind of thing that consequences relate to. Actions are best. They are identifiable, measurable, and enforceable.

Natural or Imposed?

Natural consequences are better than imposed ones. For example, if you give your teenager an allowance and she blows it on clothes, she may come to you and ask for money so she can go out with her friends. If you have told her, "This is your allowance to do with as you want, but this is all you're getting. If you want more, you'll need to get a job," then the appropriate response to her request is to say, "Sorry, honey. You chose to spend your money on clothes. Maybe next time you'll save some for going out with your friends."

Of course many of the consequences we use are somewhat artificial and imposed. This doesn't make them wrong; it only means that we are the ones who execute them. For example, if your teenager comes home after curfew, there isn't a natural consequence. You can impose a consequence by withholding car privileges or some other privilege for a while to help him learn to be more responsible.

Natural consequences are sometimes imposed by the police. I was in a town outside Port Smith, Arkansas, where I was speaking at a church. The pastor and his wife escorted me around town. They were a delightful couple and told me about their two sons. Their oldest son, who was around seventeen, had inflicted an enormous amount of hurt and pain on the family. They learned he was involved in drug use but did not know to what extent. They found out the hard way—their son was arrested for manufacturing and selling amphetamines. Due to the exposure the family received in the small town where they lived at the time, the people of the congregation accused the pastor and his wife of being bad parents and poor models for the congregation. The pastor decided it was in the best interest of the church for him to resign.

Eventually a church outside Port Smith, Arkansas, called the dad as pastor. He was thrilled, hoping the family could make a new beginning. Unfortunately, their oldest son continued the same pattern of illegal drug abuse. He got arrested again. Since he had been on probation after the first conviction, this time he was now going to be sent to a juvenile detention center.

This family was faced with a son who at first consented to getting help and at times seemed to take steps forward, but he never conquered the problem. His mom and dad were devastated, hurt, and confused and didn't know what to do. They felt they had done everything they knew to do to try to reach their son, but for whatever reason, nothing worked. Just about the time they thought the problem was resolved, their son used and sold drugs again.

This pastor and his wife were at their wit's end. Not only were they fearful of what would happen with their oldest son, they were also concerned about what kind of message was being communicated to their younger son. They asked me to meet with the son who was involved with drugs. He was still living at home while awaiting the sentencing phase of his trial. I took him to get some ice cream and asked him to tell me about his drug problem and why he had chosen the path that he'd taken. He confessed that it wasn't a relational issue or problems between him and his parents. He said his problem stemmed from peer pressure; he finally just gave in to the wrong crowd. After doing drugs for a period of time, it had become a habit. Now, as a result of repeated wrong choices, he and his entire family were facing the consequences.

The young man claimed to be a Christian, so I asked him if he realized that, due to the wrong choices he had made, he would have to reap the consequences. He replied yes; he was prepared to face them. I told him he'd have to take them head on—no matter how severe those consequences might be, no matter how inconvenient it might be, or however long it might take. He needed to realize that this was an opportunity for him to learn from the past and realize the consequences of his wrong choices.

I wanted to give him a sense of hope, so I explained that as a result of going through the pain of going to jail, he would eventually realize his family loved him deeply. The reason they pressured him to stop drugging and selling was their way of reaching out to him to help him see the truth. Now he had to face the consequences. He also needed to realize that the message this sent to his little brother was destructive and dangerous. He was deeply concerned about that, and he didn't want his little brother to end up in the same situation he was in. Finally, I stressed the fact that his parents loved him greatly, and they were the last people on earth who wanted him to reap these type of consequences. The only reason they asked me to meet with him was because of the genuine love and concern they had for him. His sinful, destructive actions did not diminish God's love or change his attitude toward him. He needed to realize that.

God used that time in the juvenile detention center for him to reflect upon his past, seek help, and get counsel. Through the entire process, this young man grew spiritually and emotionally. When he returned home, there were adjustments and awkwardness, but the family was able to put the broken pieces back together. As a result of time and healing, the family is now moving on.

The new church embraced these dear parents and provided support throughout the trauma of the arrest, trial, and imprisonment. A group of people prayed daily for them and gave them much-needed encouragement. As a result of that kind of support from the church and from close friends, this couple was able to stay strong in their faith, believing that God was going to answer prayer and bring healing to the family.

While the older son was imprisoned, the other family members grew closer together. They worked through the problems and saw how they affected each of them. Mom was able to reveal to her husband and younger son how deeply she had been hurt. The father, too, expressed his frustration, anger, and despair. Even the younger son expressed some confusion and fear to his parents. Through the process of seeking help and counsel, God was able to strengthen them. These godly parents held on to each other and their faith, and they kept believing God was going to perform a miracle in the life of their son. God answered that prayer.

After the son returned home, the family talked like they had never talked before. They were painfully honest, and it was a deeply healing experience for all of them. Over time, they established new guidelines and regained the trust that was once lost. God brought growth, healing, and a new beginning.

Common Consequences

When I speak to churches and conferences, many parents come up to me and ask, "What do we do when...?" They are looking for specific requirements and consequences for their teenager's situation. There is no magic formula to setting requirements and consequences, but here are some suggestions. I hope they give you a guideline, or at least a starting point, to finding the one that best fits your family.

Being on Time

We'll start with an easy one. A friend of mine told me his fourteen-year-old son has a mind of his own. He consistently was late getting to the car so his mother could take him and his sister to school. After months of threats and promises, this dad finally had had enough. He said, "James, if you aren't in the car by 7:50 in the morning, your mother is going to leave without you. Your bicycle is in the garage." Sure enough, the next morning James decided to test his parents' resolve. He wasn't there, so his dad told his mother to leave without him. James came down a little after eight o'clock. (He wondered why his parents hadn't called him three or four times like they usually did.) When he saw that his mother had left, he fussed and fumed for a while, then he got on his bike and rode three miles to school. The next morning he was late again. In fact, he was late every day for two weeks. During that time he sulked around the house, hoping to elicit his parents' (or at least his mother's) compassion so they would back down. The dad had to continually reassure his wife that they were doing the right thing, until she finally felt a bit more comfortable with the process. Now, months later, James is much more punctual in the mornings, but when he is late, you will find him on his bicycle, riding to school.

Curfew

Some parents set a curfew for their teenagers that includes a requirement and a consequence: if they are going to be late for any reason, they must call before the curfew; if they are late without a valid excuse (earthquakes, alien invasion, etc.), they must be home ten minutes early for every one minute they are late, and this lasts for two weeks. If this becomes a chronic problem, they may add restrictions on the car privileges to up the ante.

Car

Many parents require their children to pay for all the gas and to make sure the car is in excellent condition, including being washed and with a full tank, when it is returned. Other parents require their kids to pay for at least a portion of their part of the insurance premium each month as a requirement for using the car. If they fail to fill up the car or return it clean, they either have to do additional chores around the house, or car privileges are curtailed for a while. A friend of mine also required his son to pay for half the deductible when his son had an accident.

Finances

Some parents give their kids all the money they could ever need. I think that is a mistake. Buying love is not a good idea. I believe it is best to give your teenager a modest allowance that is tied to accomplishing chores around the house. Many parents want to instill a work ethic in their children, so they give no allowance at all after age sixteen. The teenagers must work to earn money or go without. If you give your teenager an allowance, be sure it is not a bottomless well of additional requests and doles. Make it clear that when it's spent, it's gone. That will teach budgeting and responsibility, and perhaps it will lead to a job to make some extra cash. Discretionary money is very important for young people to learn what is valuable, but of course, you can set some limits even on that. A lady I know found that her son was using his sizable allowance to buy drugs, so she cut his allowance back considerably. A few parents give their kids a credit card and pay the charges each month without asking for an accounting of the expenses. This approach does not teach financial responsibility. If you choose to give your teenager a credit card, consider letting them pay for it out of an allowance. If they overcharge the account, you will have to decide whether to let them suffer a bad credit report or let you pay it off and have them return the credit card to you.

Grades

It frustrates the stew out of parents who watch bright kids do poorly at school. If this is an aberration caused by some difficulty in his life, the teenager usually springs back to normal performance when the difficulty is resolved. If, however, the low grades persist, it may be a sign of a deeper problem, perhaps depression, which steals joy and motivation. Try to determine if there is something going on that is robbing your teenager of a sense of purpose, and address that problem directly. If a teenager has slipped into a pattern of lethargy, though, it's time to give some external motivation. Many parents use both rewards and punishments in this case. They offer perks with the car or curfew if the child brings his grades up an average of one grade point, and they withhold some privilege if he doesn't. One question some parents ask is whether to administer this consequence for the entire next grading period. My answer is: do whatever it takes to get the point across. You can negotiate, but poor performance needs to bring some pain to motivate a kid who has become a bum.

Interracial Dating

You might want to skip this one, but it is a reality for today's teenagers, especially in city schools. The United States has become a melting pot like never before, and interracial dating and marriage has become far more commonplace than it was a few years ago. Even the television commercials of some mainstream companies now feature interracial couples, and these commercials and MTV have become the model for the youth culture. Some parents are aghast that their children are even exposed to this kind of relationship, and they can't fathom their children actually dating someone from a different race. Their message is: "Absolutely not! Not in my lifetime!" But their teenagers' attitude is, "Hey, it's no big deal. Get over it." My advice is to talk about it as much as you need to, but if you strictly forbid it, interracial dating will become more desirable to your kids. Forbidden fruit tastes sweeter. Talk to your teenager about the added stress mixed marriages put on the husband and wife to fit into two cultures, and ask them what those who date across racial lines find so attractive. You might want to express the opinion that being friends with those of other races is great, and group dating is acceptable, but if teenagers are thinking of marrying someone of a different race, they need to take plenty of time to get to know the person, the culture, and themselves.

Fighting and Gangs

The school system and perhaps the police may get involved if your teenager is engaged in physical violence and gang activity. These activities are signs that something is very wrong in the person's heart. Some deep needs for security are being played out in destructive ways. Fighting for both boys and girls might be a way to prove one's toughness in the eyes of others, but there are plenty of ways a young person can channel his or her energies that are more acceptable and productive. If fighting is a habit, take the opportunity to look beneath the surface and see what the needs are. If you just try to push a fighter into the corner, he or she will fight even more. Some parents get school officials involved in surveillance to keep an eye on a kid or a gang. I encourage you to get all the help you can to turn your child around, including professional help.

Drinking and Drugs

Many young people experiment with alcohol and marijuana. In fact, just this morning a mother called to tell me that her fifteen-year-old son told her that he has decided to try a joint. He said he wants to do it at home with her permission, but if she refuses, he'll do it anyway. What would you do? I told her there are no hard and fast rules for something like this, but there are thousands of parents who would be thrilled for their kids to experiment with a joint in the safety of their home instead of out in the car with friends. Your teenagers are exposed to people who drink and use drugs all day every day if they go to public schools, and in most Christian schools too.

Instead of simply saying you forbid it, I suggest you talk about how you've seen alcohol and drugs ruin lives. A friend of mine told his two teenagers that if they ever used drugs or drank, they could forget about using the car for two months, and if they rode in the car with anyone who was drinking or using drugs, the same consequence applied. He offered to pick them up from anywhere at anytime if they call and need a ride home. No questions asked. You might want to take your son or daughter to a state institution to see patients who have fried their brains on drugs, or share stories of people you know whose lives—their marriages, their relationships with their families, their careers, and their health—have been wrecked by drinking and using. This can be a reality check for many teens.

Criminal Activity

Selling drugs, vandalism, stealing, and other forms of criminal behavior are serious problems that should be addressed quickly, clearly, and thoroughly. Some parents have asked me if they should turn their teenager in to the police. The important question to ask instead is: How can I help this person I love the most? Ignoring it or making empty threats simply don't work. One father sat down with his son who had shoplifted from a department store and told him, "I'm going to give you one day to take the stuff back and meet with the manager on your own to apologize. I will call him tomorrow at 11 o'clock to ask him how your meeting went. If he hasn't seen you,

I'm calling the police to turn you in. Do you understand?" His son got the picture, and he never shoplifted again.

Some of us don't think about it, but underage drinking and possession of drugs is a crime, so even casual drinking by most high school students is a criminal activity.

Intervention

If your child is unresponsive and insists on self-destructive behavior, you may want to consider a therapeutic intervention to back him into a corner and force the consequences on him. My advice is to enlist the assistance of a trained counselor or pastoral counselor who has experience in this kind of work. This person will want to meet with you and your spouse, and he will want to include any other adults and young people before you meet with the wayward teenager. In this preliminary meeting, each person is asked to prepare a short statement to be given when the meeting with the teenager occurs. In these statements each person honestly states what he or she has witnessed concerning the teenager's destructive actions. A time is set for the meeting, and at the last minute the teenager is invited without telling him what is going on. When he arrives, he is confronted by the power of truth and love, and each person makes his statement. Finally, the counselor gives the consequence, which is often entrance into a treatment program that addresses the teenager's specific problem. If he goes, there is hope for recovery and reconciliation. If not, he at least knows that his secret is out and he can't hide anymore. An intervention takes skill in its execution and courage for each person to speak the truth, but it offers a wonderful opportunity for repentance.

Most of us, of course, never have to go as far as this in dealing with a defiant or depressed teenager, but it's good to know that the process is available if it comes to that.

The Ultimate Consequence

If your teenager refuses to respond to you and to the Lord, and if he is at least eighteen, you may need to consider the ultimate consequence: putting him out of the house on his own. Sometimes the only way for someone to look up is by getting to the bottom, and the most loving—as well as the most painful—thing we can do is to say, "I love you very much. I've tried everything I know to do. It appears you insist on going your own way, so I'm going to honor your wishes and let you go. Take the things you need from your room and find a place to live by tomorrow at noon. Be sure of this: my door is always open. Whenever you want to have a responsible, respectful relationship again, I'm ready."

Allies

Law enforcement, the school system, your pastor, and your extended family all may be allies in your desire to help your teenager. If you feel alone and confused, talk to a trusted friend or pastor to begin gaining insight and direction. A professional counselor may be necessary to help you understand the stresses this relationship is having on you, as well as the difficulty you experience if you and your spouse don't agree on the course of action. A school counselor can help you understand what is going on at the school in your teenager's life, and this person can help steer him in a direction that is more productive. Grandparents, aunts, and uncles may be able to speak truth and encouragement to your teenager when you seem to have lost your voice. Extended times with these family members might give a new perspective to your teenager. And of course, the police can play a pivotal role in communicating the seriousness of your child's behavior if that becomes necessary. Many parents feel alone and helpless. Find the resources you need to help you be the most effective parent you can be.

A year ago, I had to go to the courthouse to pay for a speeding ticket. As I sat in a small room with other people who had broken the law, I noticed people of all ages. I was amazed at how many of them were teenagers. A large number of these teenagers were charged with DWI (driving while intoxicated) and underage drinking.

The court was about the size of a hotel room. The judge presided up front, and we were in rows of chairs. One by one we went up to the judge, and he asked us how we wanted to plead. "Guilty with probation," "guilty with circumstance," or "not guilty" were the choices given by the judge. If you pleaded guilty with circumstance, you had to come back to the judge to explain what those circumstances were. Then your fate was determined. They called us in alphabetical order, and for some reason, they started with Z and worked backward to A. Since I was a G, I had the opportunity to observe a lot of the people.

Most of the teenagers had been in groups in their cars when they got busted. Before they were called, they were snickering and laughing and acting like the entire process was a joke. When their names were called, however, and they stood before the judge, you could see by their body language and the expression on their faces that they were embarrassed and humiliated. Each of them had an excuse to explain away why he or she had gotten caught. The whole scene brought to mind the fact that there will come a day when we will answer our roll call before the judge of heaven and plead guilty or not guilty to choices given to us. Of course, there will be no excuses then. The truth will be plain for us to see.

At least a third of the kids had their parents with them. Most of these parents were there to bail their kids out. What message does that send to the kids? Instead of letting their children reap the consequences, they were trying to smooth it out for them. These parents were not drawing the line or establishing right and wrong for their kids. They were sending a message that the laws are meaningless. In effect, they were saying, "If you've got enough money or a good enough excuse, the law is irrelevant. And if you make the wrong choice or wrong decision, it doesn't matter. Somebody will bail you out." That's the wrong message to send to a teenager. They need clear guidelines and constructive consequences.

Proverbs 22:6 (NASB) says, "Train up a child in the way he should go, and when he is old he will not turn from it." Not long ago, Michelle and I were watching our girls, Rebecca and Ashlyn, ride their bicycles. As we watched them with their training wheels, I was reminded of that verse. Parents are like training wheels. They provide the spiritual, emotional, and moral stability for their children. The training wheels are to keep the children balanced and keep them from falling offtrack or falling down. The wheels are to help prepare them to ride by themselves. The same is true with parents. They are to help their kids as they provide boundaries, guidelines, limits, support, encouragement, and balance to their children. They are also preparing their children for the future when they acquire their own balance, guidance, and direction. Parents are to help kids grow in all aspects of life to live in a mature, healthy way. Spiritually, planting the Word of God to help them is like riding a bike: once you learn how, you never forget. Once we learn to apply God's Word to our lives, we see how relative God's Word is in everyday situations.

A Closer Look

1. Have you tried to control your teenager by threats and pleas in the past? If so, what are some of the results in your life, your teenager's life, and your relationship?

2. Which of the common consequences discussed in this chapter seemed to fit your situation best? Explain.

3. List problem areas with your teenager's behavior. For each one, find a consequence that fits the guidelines described in this chapter.

Beside each guideline, write out a sentence on how you will fulfill these consequences.

Problem 1:
- Clear:
- Attainable:
- Consistent:
- Agreed upon:
- Expandable:
- Enforceable:

Problem 2:
- Clear:
- Attainable:
- Consistent:
- Agreed upon:
- Expandable:
- Enforceable:

Problem 3:
- Clear:
- Attainable:
- Consistent:
- Agreed upon:
- Expandable:
- Enforceable:

4. Who or what are some resources you might use to help you clarify the steps you need to take and help you take them?

EIGHT

MANAGING ANGER

As I have talked with parents over the last few years, one common denominator emerges in the vast majority of our conversations: they wrestle with anger, either their own or their teenager's. Angry outbursts have broken their hearts. Slammed doors have crushed their spirits. Sullen glares have stolen their hope and joy. These parents are looking for help. In this chapter, I want to look at some important principles about how to manage anger. With no apologies, we will focus this chapter on the parents because if parents can manage their own anger, they can model and teach these valuable truths to their children. If, however, parents can't internalize these insights, no amount of preaching and teaching, even good and biblical principles, will have a positive impact on their teenagers. Kids need to see it before they buy it.

The battleground in anger management is not in the emotions; it is in the mind. Our thoughts are shaped by what we believe about ourselves, about God, and about other people in our lives. Learning to think rightly is the goal and the process of anger management.

What Is Anger?

Anger is a reaction to a threat, real or perceived. When someone's words or actions threaten our security or significance, our bodies or our property, we get angry. Similarly, when we feel that someone is unreasonably demanding a certain reaction from us, we react in anger. Some of us are so insecure that we can't afford to lose even a skirmish, let alone a war. We have to be right, all the time, in all ways, in front of all people. This unrealistic demand reveals a deep insecurity that is easily and often threatened.

Many psychologists have observed that anger is a surface emotion. It is the one that is visible; but underneath may be fear, hurt, and loneliness. When a person fears being rejected, he more readily lashes out at anyone or anything that may even remotely make him feel vulnerable. In many families this threat is only too real, so the fear is often realized and reinforced. The problem is that this person often generalizes the fear to include not only the few who actually use intimidation to control him, but he believes that every person he encounters has these insidious motives. He becomes afraid and threatened by almost everybody.

We are creatures of habit, and habits shape our families. Many of us are consumed by emotions today because we have experienced the same events over and over again for decades. We seem locked in an emotional prison, and the key is nowhere to be found. For example, a woman who had an emotionally distant father suffered under the belief that she couldn't do enough to please her dad. She tried as hard as she could to win his approval, but nothing worked. Her life was a constant effort to please him, dotted by outbursts of rage at his inattention, then guilt for feeling so selfish. Her hurt and anger were reinforced every day by his disconnection and his lack of love and support for her. As a grown woman, she married a man who is similarly emotionally absent. A psychologist might conclude that she married him because she either still needed to work out her childhood hurts or she simply felt more comfortable with someone who didn't demand vulnerability from her. However, the reason she married him is not the point. The hurts she experienced as a child continue to be felt over and over again as an adult. Whatever the cause, the hurts, the belief that she is unworthy of love, and her own angry outbursts are repeated year to year, and in her relationship with her son—generation to generation.

As we saw in earlier chapters, anger isn't sin. Paul instructed the Ephesian believers to "be angry but do not sin" (Eph. 4:26 RSV). The feeling of anger, however, can be channeled in two ways: toward resolution or toward revenge. There is, I believe, tremendous energy in our anger. It can be used as a force for good or as a force for evil. That is our choice. If we use it to speak truth and to take constructive steps to define responsibilities and find solutions, that energy is a force for good. Yet if we lapse into gossip, name calling, cursing, snarling, blaming, and any of the host of other ways we try to hurt those who have hurt us, we sin against God and against that person. James observed this way that we destructively act out our anger when he wrote, "For man's anger does not bring about the righteous life that God desires" (James 1:20). If we use our anger's energy to seek God and a solution, God is honored, and each person involved can grow stronger and wiser. On the other hand, if we use our anger to intimidate, control, or isolate, we disobey the one who bought us, and we harm ourselves and those around us. The emotion of anger isn't wrong, but our actions in response to it are either righteous or evil.

Interpretation, Please

Most of us don't have much objectivity about our thought patterns. We don't have sensors in our minds that signal "Alert!" when we are thinking incorrectly, but we need to develop those sensors. They are absolutely vital when learning to manage our anger. The apostle Paul talked about right thinking as a war. He wrote, "For though we live in the world, we do not wage war as the world does. The weapons we fight with are not the weapons of the world. On the contrary, they have divine power to demolish strongholds. We demolish arguments and every pretension that sets itself up against the knowledge of God, and we take captive every thought to make it obedient to Christ" (2 Cor. 10:3–5).

If anger rules your life, it has become a stronghold, both emotionally and spiritually. How is a stronghold destroyed? Paul says it is by demolishing it—taking direct action to identify it, gather resources, and attack it. Strongholds aren't destroyed by wishing they'd go away. In Paul's day siege warfare was often practiced against a city. For months and even years, the attacking army battered the walls of the city and approached closer and closer until the walls were breached. In the same way, our false beliefs about ourselves, God, and others need to be identified and attacked with tenacity and strength. Let's identify some of the false beliefs that can trigger our anger.

"I need this person's love and acceptance to feel good about myself." As we will see, most of the beliefs that plague us are rooted in externals. We believe we aren't sufficient in ourselves, so we have to have someone else's approval. When it comes, we feel good . . . until it vanishes, or we fear it will vanish. When we don't receive it, we feel hurt and angry at the one who denied us.

"I feel controlled, and I don't like it!" When we are dependent on others' approval, we are easily controlled by their words and moods. If they are happy, we can be happy. If they aren't happy, it must be our fault. If they want something, we jump to make it happen in the hope that we'll get that cherished "attaboy!" we crave.

"If God loved me, he'd make things work out better for me." Ultimately, our anger is directed toward God. We believe his job is to make us happy, and we are angry at him when he fails to perform his duties. Some of us are well aware of our anger toward God, but for others, this realization is simply too threatening. We can't admit we are angry at God, just as we can't admit we are angry at our parents. We choose to live in the illusion that we aren't angry at all.

"If he changes, I can be happy." Our hopes and happiness are rooted in the life of the other person. We believe that if he would just come to his senses and change his life, everything would be wonderful; life would be great. We fail to realize that living according to externals always makes us vulnerable and easily threatened.

"I'm a victim. I deserve better." Some people have experienced great difficulties: abuse, neglect, abandonment, and other deep emotional wounds. We are victims, but haven't healed. Being (and remaining) a victim creates a strong sense of entitlement; we are convinced we deserve better. In fact, other people and God owe us peace, love, and security! And we demand it . . . right now! When others fail to come through—and this happens all the time—we get furious at them.

"I'm a victim, but I don't deserve better. I'm scum." Some of us have internalized the hurts and concluded that we don't deserve anything good from anyone, including God. We live in a permanent state of depression, which in most cases can be described as "anger turned inward."

"Everything is a crisis." Angry, insecure people make mountains out of molehills. The slightest inconvenience is an offense. An insignificant slight creates an explosion of hurt and anger.

"If I think about it enough, it'll get better." Some of us analyze every word and action of every minute of every day, hoping to find someone to blame for the injustices. Our lives are consumed by finding fault because, after all, someone must take the heat for everything that goes wrong. The problem is that much of this morbid introspection is turned inward, and we caustically blame ourselves for everything we say and do, even the good things.

These are but a few of the faulty interpretations people have about life. They lead to beliefs that the world is out to get us, and we feel terribly threatened. Sometimes these threats are very real, but sometimes they are imagined. Quite often, small threats are seen through the lenses of past hurts, which causes them to be blown far out of proportion with reality.

Ways We Deal with Anger

I met two sisters a few years ago. One of them was a confident and commanding person. She was very blunt and took charge of any situation. If there was a problem of any kind, she stepped up to handle it. People had great respect for her. The other sister was always smiling. No matter what happened, her response almost universally was to smile and say, "That's nice." As I got to know these girls and saw these two patterns of behavior day after day, I realized something strange was happening. I asked a few questions and found out there was tremendous stress in their family. Each girl had chosen a different way to cope with that stress. One tried to avoid pain by controlling everybody and everything, and the other tried to eliminate her pain by avoiding conflict at all costs. The girl who was so sweet and kind and smiling all the time had what some psychologists call "smiling depression." She didn't walk around moping all the time, but beneath the smiles she was really depressed.

Which of these two girls got the love that they desperately wanted? Neither one. One earned respect—or fear—from those she trampled on, but respect and fear aren't love. The other evoked pity from the people around her, but that certainly isn't love either. Neither of these girls got what she wanted. They both were looking for love while trying to avoid pain at all costs, but they were settling for a substitute: one for respect, the other for pity. Neither met their needs.

Stress and anger are very closely related, so the observations we made in previous chapters about the ways people cope apply here as well. For the sake of clarity, let me outline some of the most common ways we handle our anger.

We suppress it. Some of us feel so threatened by the idea of expressing our anger that we stuff it inside. A few of us won't admit we are hurt or angry or that we feel offended in any way. More of us admit that we feel hurt and angry, but our conclusion is, "I'm a terrible person. I must have done something very wrong to bring this on myself." We keep stuffing it as long as we can.

We explode. Some of us are like a string of lit firecrackers. We go off time after time when we're exposed to just a little heat. Others are more like volcanoes; we keep the lid on for a long time as the hot lava of anger and bitterness builds, then we explode in a fit of rage.

We are passive aggressive. I don't believe anybody is truly passive. We find some way to express our anger, and for some of us, that expression has become a subtle art form. We gossip with the intent of hurting the person's reputation, and if we are caught, we insist with faked innocence, "I didn't mean to hurt anybody." Or if the person is a family member, we find out what drives him crazy, and we do it over and over again. For instance, if your husband is punctual, you might delay getting ready. How long do you make him wait? Probably just long enough for his blood pressure to boil but not so long that it becomes obvious you are punishing him on purpose. When he asks for the third time, "Are you ready yet?" you say, "Just one more minute. I can't find the right belt for this outfit." Ten minutes later you finally walk out the door, and he sighs heavily. You've won the battle. He's upset about being late, but your excuse is intact.

We escape. A common response to a threat is to get away as far as possible as quickly as possible. We might try to avoid conflict by giving in to whatever demands anyone might have so that we get the tension over quickly. Some of us use drugs or alcohol to numb the pain, while others use television, pornography, shopping, or anything else that takes up the space in our hearts and on our schedules so we don't have to feel the hurt and anger.

We prove ourselves. Because many of us are determined not to feel pain ever again, not to lose control, and not to let anyone intimidate us, we strive to be on top—to dominate others and prove our worth. We may do this through business ventures, by developing a commanding personality, or through involvement in clubs, hobbies, or anything else that lets us excel.

We have moral lapses. Some of us give up. We have tried to make sense of life for a long, long time, and it just hurts too badly. We find solace in the arms of someone who promises passion without demands. It sounds good, and it actually feels good for a while, but eventually we are left empty again—even more hurt, angry, and lonely than before.

We have poor health. We may get high on the adrenalin rush of anger, but we pay a high price for the experience. The most common spots where we pay for long-term unresolved anger are in our stomachs, heads, and shoulders. Some of us live with nearly constant headaches, stomach and intestinal upsets, and tense muscles because our bodies are uptight from the stress of being angry so often.

We resolve it. There is a better way. Instead of all these unproductive ways of trying to cope with our anger, we can learn to think rightly, control our emotions, and choose behaviors that are productive for ourselves and for those in our lives. What's more, these ways honor the Lord too. The first step is to learn new, improved ways of thinking and interpreting our circumstances so that the flow of anger and retribution is stopped.

Right Thinking

The introduction to John's Gospel tells us that Jesus came to bring us grace and truth. Not one or the other—both. Right thinking is founded on both of those powerful qualities, and the principles we learn can transform our lives and our relationships with those around us. Some of these principles are easily recognized, and we need to embrace them instead of shaking our heads at them. Others may be revolutionary to some of us. Let's examine some of the pillar principles of right thinking.

My emotions are the product of my thoughts and beliefs.

We may seem locked into feeling the same things over and over again and think that change is hopeless. The solution is not, "Just don't feel that way!" but instead, "Learn to think differently." The battle, as you recall, is won in our minds, not in our emotions.

I can't control others.

Lord knows we've tried! Some of us have spent our lives trying to control the behaviors of others, to get them to love us, or to get them to act in ways that reflect well on us. The only person we can control is ourselves. For the rest of the six billion people on this planet, we need to give them choices and let them respond. If they choose to take a step toward us in truth, reconciliation, and trust, that's great. But if they choose to walk away or condemn us, there is at least integrity in letting them make that decision. I believe most of us control (or try to control) others because we are afraid they will, indeed, walk away, and we simply don't think we can stand that. A part of this truth, then, is to have a new sense of our own security.

I am loved, forgiven, and accepted in Christ.

Our security is not rooted in people; it is found on the bedrock of the gospel of Jesus Christ. We are fallen but redeemed. We have sinned, but Jesus died to pay for those sins so we can be forgiven. Like the father in the story of the prodigal son, God longs to shower his wayward children with his love and blessings. When you look in the mirror and ask yourself, "Who am I?" what is your answer? Many of us try to prove we are valuable by showing all that we've accomplished, but in our hearts we know others have done better. Many of us try to please people, hoping to win their love. Sometimes we get it, but even then we fear losing it. In Christ, though, we find perfect love that casts out fear, and the acceptance we've always longed for. God doesn't rescue us out of the struggles of life, but he promises to be with us every step of the way.

I can make good choices.

You aren't helpless, powerless, or worthless. You have the ability to make choices to take steps in the right direction. Some of those choices are directly against all we have valued and believed in the past, but as our thinking and beliefs change, we gain new strength.

The earliest choices of change are often the hardest, but they are absolutely crucial in charting a new course for our hearts and our relationships.

My emotions are gifts from the Lord.

Some of us despise our fears, hurts, and anger, but there is nothing wrong with the feelings at all. They are the flashing signals on the dashboards of our lives. They tell us we need to pay attention because something's wrong. Instead of seeing these feelings as hindrances to health and wholeness, see them as doorways to find God's peace and truth.

I don't have to be right.

One of the greatest statements in the annals of human experience is "I was wrong." Some of us have never admitted we are wrong, so we have stopped the experience of forgiveness and restoration before it began. The compulsion to be right is rooted in the fear that someone will hurt us. It is the need to control ourselves, our circumstances, and everyone around us. Ultimately, however, it isolates us and leaves us empty and heartbroken. Admitting our faults, errors, and sins is a wonderful step toward honesty and truth. Even the apostle Paul, probably the strongest believer in the history of the church, admitted he was "chief" of sinners before he found grace (see 1 Tim. 1:15 KJV). And as a believer, he confessed, "I do not understand what I do. For what I want to do I do not do, but what I hate I do" (Rom. 7:15). In fact, the realization of his sinfulness brought his despairing comment, "What a wretched man I am! Who will rescue me from this body of death?" (Rom. 7:24). His honesty led him to pen one of the most inspiring and comforting passages in the Bible. He wrote, "Thanks be to God—through Jesus Christ our Lord! . . . Therefore, there is now no condemnation for those who are in Christ Jesus" (Rom. 7:25–8:1). If Paul can admit his need for God's grace, you and I can admit ours too.

I will assign appropriate responsibility.

As we learn to think correctly, one of the skills we acquire is to determine what we are responsible for and what we aren't. We will be able to see that we are responsible for our own choices, our expressions of emotions, and our behaviors. We'll also see that other people are responsible for theirs. This assignment of responsibility clarifies much of the confusion we have experienced; therefore, we have more peace because we aren't trying to control things we can't control.

I have found that it takes time and hard work to change my thinking patterns. How I think is so deeply rooted in me that it genuinely requires a siege mentality (remember 2 Cor. 10:3–5?) to overcome the patterns of the past. I read, I study the Scriptures, and I talk to trusted friends to get insights. Little by little new insights emerge. New beliefs gradually replace the old ones, and new behaviors crowd out the old, destructive ones. I wish there was a pill to take to make it easier, but if there were, we wouldn't appreciate the riches of the truth when we found it. Right thinking requires tenacity and firmness of spirit, much like mining for gold or besieging a city. In both cases, those involved get tired and sometimes want to quit, but if they continue, they can achieve something they've wanted their whole lives.

STEPS TO TAKE

Based on all we have seen in these pages, let me offer five steps to take to manage your anger.

Step 1: Watch for Triggers.

What are the flashing signals on the dashboard of your life? Do you clench your teeth? Does your head feel like a steel band is gripping it? Do you have constant stomach pains . . . or worse? Do you find yourself cursing for seemingly no reason at all? Do you have problems sleeping or eating (too much or too little)? Don't explain these signals away any longer. Let them be doorways you walk through to find truth and grace. As you do, look for the ways you have tried to cope with your anger and hurt (suppressing it, exploding, passive-aggressive behavior, etc.) and say, "That's me. I do that." Admit it. Embrace it. Truth is the way to healing and strength.

Step 2: Reinterpret Reality.

Ask yourself, "What am I believing right now?" Look back over the thought patterns described in this chapter and identify those that have shackled you. If you can identify them, you can make the choice to change your thoughts. Sometimes we need to reinterpret reality in the middle of a heated conversation. In that case, call time-out. Say, "I need a few minutes to think through what you're saying. Let's get back together in about fifteen minutes." Whatever it takes to identify the faulty thought patterns and choose new ones, do it!

Memorize passages of Scripture and statements like the ones listed in this chapter. Having them in your head and in your heart is essential if you want to use them to fight the errant beliefs effectively. I also encourage you to write down Scripture verses that are helpful to you. According to Jewish custom, people actually bound the truth of the Scriptures to their foreheads, and many Orthodox Jews still use little boxes called phylacteries to keep these bits of the Bible strapped to their foreheads. I urge you to find the best way for you to focus on the truth so you internalize it day in and day out, in good times and in conflict.

Step 3: Make Good Choices.

Instead of reacting in explosions or demands, by running away or giving in, make good and godly choices based on the truth you have learned. Select a good time and place to communicate the truth, but realize that you probably won't feel warm and fuzzy about speaking the truth to someone you've feared for many years. The choice is to *do* the right thing, not necessarily to *feel* the right thing. That may be beyond your control. In most cases, we have to fight through our feelings in order to do what is right.

Use word choices that are good and right. Don't blame, and don't get into name calling. Use the "I feel, I want, I will" formula for successful communication, and remember not to judge yourself by the other person's response. (Look at how people responded to Jesus, and he communicated with the ultimate in grace and truth.) Give the person time to decide what to do. Too often, we demand that a person respond immediately, but that is unrealistic in many cases. When asking someone for a response to a choice, give him a day or two to think about it. Then his choice will reflect his reason (however flawed it may be), not his passions of the moment.

Step 4: Be Clear.

The fog of confusion has blanketed many of our hearts. These five steps and the insights we gain are designed to lift that fog so our thoughts, our beliefs, and even our emotions are clearer. Clarifying our thoughts takes work. We have to blast the old ones before we can build the new patterns. Repentance is based on a clear evaluation of what is wrong and a grasp of what is good. Take time to read and reread books and articles so you develop a new system of thought. Talk to a trusted friend, a pastor, or a counselor to get the help you need. We all need outside input to give us objectivity about the things we hold most dear, especially our false beliefs. There have been times in my life when a friend has given me insights that I would never have gained on my own, no matter how much time and effort I put into finding truth. Don't feel that you are alone. Get the help you need.

Clarity of thought does not ensure clarity of emotions. In fact, when we realize we've been headed in the wrong direction for many years, change is terribly threatening. Fears are increased, not diminished. Hold fast to the truth as Abraham did when he trusted God to make him the father of a great nation even though his wife had been infertile for so many years, or as Noah did when he built the ark over many years even though there was no rain. Cling to the truth even when it is dark and difficult. Light will come eventually.

Step 5: Be Strong.

"Fear not" is used 365 times in the Scriptures. That long litany of admonitions must mean one thing: we are often tempted to give in to our fears. God told Joshua to "be strong and very courageous" (Josh. 1:7) as he led the children of Israel into the promised land. Joshua felt overwhelmed and afraid, but God gave him a command to be strong and not to waver.

Reinforce the truth in your mind and heart at every occasion. Sing songs about God's faithfulness and grace. Memorize Scripture and statements that affirm your strength and God's grace. Pray with passion that God will work in your heart to give you eyes to see the truth and then give you the strength to do it. Focus on your own responsibility, not on changing the other people who grieve you. Make amends to those you've wronged. Say those three little words, "I was wrong," and ask for forgiveness. When you are weak, then you are strong.

Monitor your emotions and your thoughts. Be a student of your mind so you can determine which thoughts need to be enhanced and which ones need to be changed. If you find yourself exploding or imploding, back away and give yourself time to think more clearly.

* * *

Managing your anger is one of the most courageous and profitable things you can do for yourself and for your family. You may have picked up this book with the goal of managing your teenager's anger, but my suggestion is that you start a little closer to home—in your own heart. In the next chapter, we will examine some principles for building a more positive environment in your home.

A Closer Look

1. Think of the last three times you felt angry. What was the threat (real or perceived) you were responding to?
   1. _____
   2. _____
   3. _____

2. Have you been taught that anger is sin? If so, how has that affected your willingness to admit you are angry? How has that affected your honesty with God about your emotions?

3. Look over the list of common interpretations of threats on pages 114–115. Which of these apply to you? How have they kept you a prisoner of anger?

4. Look at the list of how we cope with anger. Which of these applies most closely to your experience? Which applies to your spouse? To your teenager?

5. Which of the statements of right thinking is hardest to believe? Explain.

6. Think of the last three times you were angry. How would following the steps to manage anger have helped you in each one?
   1. _____
   2. _____
   3. _____

NINE

A REDUCED-STRESS ENVIRONMENT

Do you remember the story of Rachel in chapter 5? She was the sweet young woman who got involved with a young man and got pregnant. When we last saw Rachel and her parents, they had just heard the news, and they were devastated. Rachel had some choices to make. Over the next several days, their heads spun like tops as they tried to figure out what the best course might be. Everyone thought abortion was out of the question—except for Richard. He told Rachel to get it done quickly. He wanted the nuisance of a baby out of his life. This response should have told Rachel all she needed to know about the young man she had hoped would give her the love she wanted, but the synapses didn't connect. She was still too much under his spell. She continued to spend every waking moment with him, while her parents agonized as much over her blindness as they did over the consequences and confusion caused by her poor choices.

Everyone had advice for Rachel and her parents. Many people suggested she should marry Richard, and as many more told her to stay single and give the child up for adoption. A few quietly mentioned that abortion wasn't so bad in some cases, and this was one of those cases. As time dragged on, the decision about the baby began to take a backseat to the sick, binding grip Richard had on Rachel. Her parents knew she had to break free of him or she would endure abuse and bitterness far greater than anything she had experienced thus far. They found a home for unwed mothers, sponsored by a Christian group, in Virginia. They called to get as much information as possible, and they found that the home would take Rachel as soon as she could get there. God, it seemed, had provided a wonderful place for Rachel to have the child and begin to rebuild her life. No, she wouldn't have the storybook experience of going to college, meeting Mr. Right, and falling in love as all had expected, but under the circumstances, this was an enormous answer to prayer.

There was only one problem: Rachel wanted to stay with Richard. For weeks her parents pleaded with her to go to Virginia. They painted a picture of the kind of life she would have with Richard if she stayed, and their bleak picture was based on fact. They learned that Richard had physically assaulted Rachel on several occasions, and many times he had kept her a virtual prisoner in his apartment, not allowing her to leave or call home to let her parents know where she was.

Depression gripped the entire family as Rachel's emotional shackles got tighter and tighter. She seemed incapable of thinking for herself. She was Richard's slave, but she didn't want to be free. Finally, after a month of agony, her parents told her, "We're buying you a plane ticket to Virginia. If you go, there's hope that you can find peace and joy with your new child. If you stay with Richard, you will know only heartache and depression. Your child will have a demanding, abusive father, and that will have been your choice. If you leave, we will support you in every way we possibly can, but if you stay, you are on your own. We will love you and pray for you every day we are alive, but we will not support your decision to be with Richard. Do you understand?"

Rachel somehow understood that this was not an empty threat. Her parents meant every word, and she knew it. The plane ticket was purchased for the next Saturday, and her mother put it on her dresser. Every day Rachel left home early to be with Richard, and she stayed with him all day until about 2:00 the next morning. Hope faded that week for her parents, and the hopeless look on Rachel's face didn't offer any solace that her decision to be with Richard held any promise of happiness whatsoever. On Friday night, Rachel told her parents that she had decided to go to Virginia. They were thrilled, and her mother helped her pack her things. Suddenly the phone rang. Richard wanted her to go out that night. Rachel hesitated a few minutes and then offered a lame excuse. Richard didn't buy it, and he convinced her to go out with him. Rachel's parents feared he would change her mind. She hadn't even told Richard she was thinking of leaving. If she did, he would put a major guilt trip on her and convince her to stay. Now, her parents feared she would tell him, and she would be at his controlling, manipulative mercy.

The next morning, fear and hope in equal measure gripped the household, but when Richard came by at 9 o'clock, Rachel went out the door with him. All seemed lost, and the parents sank into their deepest despair. The plane was to leave at 2:00 in the afternoon, but Rachel was gone without a word about coming back. The clock ticked slowly all morning. Rachel's mother tried to do housework to pass the time, but she was in agony. Rachel's father worked in the garage, but he too couldn't keep his mind off the momentous decision of the day. His head pounded from the stress, but no amount of aspirin helped.

Around noon, Rachel came in the door and announced, "Who's going to take me to the airport?" Her parents almost wept with joy and excitement. Yes, they were sending their precious daughter a thousand miles away—possibly for the rest of her life—so she could stay away from this predator, but it was the best option available to her. They grabbed her bags and headed to the airport. On the way, Rachel's expression changed. She vacillated and wondered if she was doing the right thing. A knot gripped her mother's stomach, and her father's headache returned. They read her body language on the thirty-minute drive to the airport. Every motion and every sigh was analyzed. Fears and hopes fought every mile of the way. Finally, they arrived at the curb. Rachel's father parked the car as her mother walked with her to the ticket counter so she could check her bags. Her father parked in warp speed so he could get back to make sure she didn't change her mind. The three of them waited at the gate for about twenty minutes, not saying much, but knowing everything had already been said a thousand times before. Would she change her mind again? The airline attendant called her row of seats, and Rachel stood up, took a deep breath, and hugged her parents. Now a flood of tears filled their eyes as they said goodbye. Rachel turned and walked down to the plane. And she was gone.

Her parents felt incredible joy and sadness at the same time. Relief and anger. Hurt and hope. They had prayed so hard that she would leave, but their little girl was leaving them. What would happen to her now? What would happen to them now?

Many stories don't have happy endings, but this is one of the most rewarding stories I've heard in a long time. When Rachel got to Virginia, she was welcomed warmly by the staff and other young women at the home. In the next few weeks, her spirit, crushed by two years of abuse and condemnation, now began to come back to life. She laughed again. She began to think for herself again. Her calls to her parents began to be filled with insight and hope. She became furious at Richard—and at herself for being so stupid to believe his lies and let herself be manipulated. Her anger was good and right, and the staff at the home helped her grieve all she had lost.

But she had also gained something very precious. About six months after she arrived at the home, Rachel gave birth to a darling little girl. "I know I made dumb decisions," she told her proud parents, "but I wouldn't trade anything for Sarah. She's a gift from God."

Today Rachel is doing very well, actually, incredibly well. Getting away from Richard allowed her to become herself again. In fact, she is more than she ever was before. She is again a sweet girl, but now she is wise and savvy. Her fears are being replaced with confidence, and her blind trust of a predator has been replaced by insight and caution. She has new friends as well as a fresh, vital relationship with God. Not long ago, Rachel's parents despaired that she would ever smile again, but today she is a confident, relaxed, energetic single mother with a bright future.

Rachel and her parents look back on that day when they stopped pleading and threatening and gave her a clear choice: go or stay; leave with our support or stay without it. We will love you either way, but there are consequences for your decision. That day her choice became clear. It was still excruciatingly difficult, and she wavered terribly, but at least it was clear. And she took it.

Stress-Reduced, Not Stress-Free

As parents deal with their own hurts, anger, and stress, they will be able to clarify choices for their teenagers. This process, however, doesn't bring immediate peace. On the contrary, the initial stages of change often bring more turmoil than ever before. We are creatures of habit, and even if things are bad, most of us prefer them to stay the way they are instead of changing. This disdain for change was expressed by someone this way, "My life may be hell, but at least I know the names of the streets." Change brings confusion and stress, but it offers the only way of hope.

As you implement the principles in this book, you can expect your teenager (and perhaps your spouse) to "kick against the goads"

(Acts 26:14). You may see clearly how this process will ultimately lead to healing and good communication, but they may not want to take those steps. In this chapter, I want to offer some suggestions to help you make it through this time and come out on the other side with lower stress levels, warmer communication, and more affection and affirmation than ever before. But remember, you can't control others' responses. You can only do the right thing and let them decide how to react.

SHARE THE PRINCIPLES

Take time to tell your family the things you are learning, mostly about yourself, and perhaps about the family's way of dealing with stress and anger. Don't identify each person's particular sins in this process! Focus on your own faulty thinking, errant coping behaviors, and your hopes for the future. Don't lecture, but share what you are learning.

Model the anger management principles. Modeling them is far more powerful than lecturing your family on them. Be sure to say, "I was wrong. Please forgive me." when you mess up. (If you don't say it at least once a day, you are either a hermit or still in denial!) You might want to talk to your family about one or two of the faulty beliefs and the right-thinking statements listed in chapter 8. Tell how the faulty beliefs have hindered you, disappointed you, and kept you from being the person God wants you to be, and talk about how refreshing it is to have a new handle on right thoughts. Again, focus on what *you* are learning and how these principles are helping you. Don't preach.

Ask your family to hold you accountable. A friend of mine told his daughter, "You know, I've had a problem with trying to control people, telling them what to do. [She nodded affirmingly.] But I want to learn to stop doing that. It will be really hard because that's all I've ever known to do, so I need your help. Would you tell me whenever you feel that I am trying to control you? I'd appreciate it if you'd do that. If I try to defend myself, call me on that too, OK?"

A smile crept across his daughter's face. "Sure, Dad," she told him. "I'll be glad to do that." And she did. Over the next few months, his daughter told him on several occasions, "Dad, you're doing that control thing again." He wanted to blame her, and he wanted to walk out in a huff, but he swallowed hard and said, "OK. You're right. I sure am. Please forgive me. Thanks for telling me. I'll try to do better next time."

This honesty and integrity did wonders for both of them. His daughter was being treated like an adult, and he respected her input. He was being honest with her, and his willingness to admit when he was wrong was a wonderful example to his daughter. I recommend this kind of family accountability very strongly.

I was speaking at a church in Austin, Texas, and at the conclusion of my talk, a broken, discouraged couple came forward to talk to me. The lady told me she was so emotional because her seventeen-year-old son had recently been convicted of manslaughter. He had killed two girls while driving under the influence of alcohol. This grieving mother came to the altar that morning along with her husband to ask for help. She unloaded all of the emotions she had been bottling up. She was bitter toward her son because of the hurt, disappointment, embarrassment, and humiliation that was brought upon the family. After hearing me talk about forgiveness that morning, she wanted desperately for God to free her of her pain. Holding on to bitterness is like holding a match; it burns the one who is holding it. I talked about how we need to let go and let God take over those emotions.

That morning God worked in her heart. She was willing to let go of those angry feelings and emotions she was holding in her heart toward her son. I watched the release of emotions as she laid them at the altar. A real spirit of genuine forgiveness came over her. She was now ready to approach her son and make things right between the two of them.

Clarify Their Choices

Our children have gotten used to us either avoiding conflict at all cost, blaming them fiercely, or fixing their problems. As we stop doing those things and learn to communicate clearly and strongly, we can clarify their choices and give them consequences. Some people have said, "Well, isn't this a form of controlling them?" My answer is no; there is a world of difference between manipulating someone and giving them choices with consequences. Controlling them puts the burden on you to make them do the right thing; giving choices puts the burden on them. Your role is to clarify these choices, communicate the rewards and punishments, support where you need to and back off where you need to, and enforce the consequences.

We have looked at dozens of different scenarios that cause problems between parents and teenagers. In most cases, young people can participate in clarifying the choices themselves. Ask, "What do you think is a good time for you to be home?" and "What should be the consequences if you are late or if you don't call?" Sometimes the kids are much more strict than the parents (and then you get to be the good guy by softening the punishment). Negotiated agreements are best, but if your teenager demands too much rope, don't be shy about saying, "No, I can't agree with two in the morning. I think eleven is late enough for a weeknight and midnight for a Friday and Saturday."

Take Action but Don't Fix

A parent should be a teenager's biggest cheerleader, but that young person needs to learn to be independent, not tied to the parent's thoughts and desires. Be supportive, but stop short of fixing your teenager's problems. Does this sound contradictory? It does if you are used to stepping in too often. Get some objective feedback from parents who have clear boundaries and have raised kids who are now independent, strong young adults. These experienced parents may have wrestled with the same difficulties you face, and they learned from it. Now they can help you.

Offer support and encouragement to your teenager but not so much that you rob him of initiative and responsibility. This balance requires you to know yourself—your compulsion to fix things in order to win love or your fear of conflict that makes you run away—and to know your teenager—his level of maturity and the way he learns. Some kids learn only the hard way—by trial and error—but some are more perceptive and learn by watching others make mistakes or succeed. As your teenager grows up, your role changes. Parenting a high school senior is quite different from parenting a freshman. One is much more independent, and the expectations and responsibilities are far higher than for younger kids. Treat each accordingly. Make adjustments to your own expectations and how you relate. For example, you are preparing the senior to be on his own in a few months. Too many restrictions, especially unrealistic ones, may well create a thirst for freedom that explodes in poor decisions when he leaves home and must make his own decisions. A wise course of action is to treat him like an adult before he leaves, which will give him necessary and valuable practice. Yet treating him like an adult still means there are negotiated boundaries and expectations.

Affirm, Affirm

As the parent of a teenager, you are under tremendous stress, but remember that your kid is under tremendous stress too. Make it a point to find things she does well every day. Affirm, affirm, affirm. Avoid name-calling and negative labeling to your teenager and about her to your friends. Don't whine and gossip about all the things your teenager is doing wrong and how she's driving you crazy. Speak to her with respect, and speak about her with respect—the way you want her to talk about you.

Some of us are so angry and hurt in this relationship that our lives are consumed with damage control. We haven't heard a kind word in months, and we've forgotten how to give them to our teenager. If this is true of you, break the pattern. Be a source of light and life. Find something (anything!) your teenager does well and affirm her each day. Look into his world and find things he values and affirm them. You may find that after a while a few kindnesses may find their way back to you. The law of reaping and sowing is universal: we reap what we sow—after we sow and more than we sow. Affirmation is a wonderful seed to sow as much as possible. It yields a crop of kindness, strength, and joy.

Learning, Not Blaming

In an environment where choices are clearer and kind words are spoken more often, our compulsion to fix blame is reduced. Some of us have been "blame sponges," soaking up everything that is wrong in the family and concluding, "It must be my fault." Our spouses and kids may have assisted in this assessment. Others of us have been "blame throwers," pointing fingers at someone else to make sure somebody besides us get the blame for what's wrong. As we heal and grow, however, fixing blame becomes less of an issue. Instead, our question becomes, "What does God want me to learn in this?" A clenched fist of anger becomes an open hand to receive God's truth and grace. That truth may be comforting, or it may be challenging, but we want to embrace it.

Our view of God gradually changes from demanding that he fix every problem or leave us alone, to a sovereign, loving Father who will use every heartache and every joy to draw us closer to himself. God is more concerned about our growth than our pleasure. If we understand that, we will look to him even in the most difficult moments and trust that he is able to give us wisdom and hope. He is able to bring light out of the deepest darkness in our lives and our families—if we trust him. Just ask Rachel and her parents. They can attest to God's gracious hand working to produce good even with the most painful raw materials and even with the most fragile faith.

Enjoy Each Other

As the tension level is reduced, you will find that molehills remain molehills. Everything is not a crisis after all! In fact, some of the things that seemed so traumatic are now minor annoyances, perhaps even trivial. We can enjoy healthy disagreements instead of having to win every encounter. We can listen and appreciate the other person's point of view, even if we disagree with it. And we laugh more together.

Look for things to enjoy together to bring joy back into the relationship. Games, a favorite family-friendly sitcom, or a hike in the mountains can be something you enjoy together. Just don't make a big deal out of doing these things in front of your teenager's friends. Let it be your family secret, or your kids may be too embarrassed to do anything else with you again—unless, of course, your teenager tells people. (OK, it's not much of a chance, but it could happen.)

In the next chapter we'll look at some habits that will change your life and your relationship with your teenager.

A Closer Look

1. Can you identify with Rachel's parents in any way? their hopes and pains? Explain.

2. Which of the false beliefs and right-thinking statements from chapter 8 are most meaningful to you? How and when can you share these with your teenager?

3. What does it mean to you to "take action but don't fix"?

4. What have you noticed in your teenager in the past few days that you can affirm? (Attitudes, talents, successes, skills, hard work, etc.)

5. What do you think God wants you to learn during this time of difficulty?

6. Is it easier to blame or to open yourself to God to learn from him? Explain.

7. What would a reduced-stress environment look like in your household?

TEN

FORGIVENESS...
AND OTHER LONGINGS

I received a letter from a young lady who heard me speak at her school. When I read her letter, I began to weep. When I speak in schools, I ask myself if I'm really making a difference. Is my message sinking in and getting through? Am I connecting with these young people? Is it making a lasting difference? This letter is a snapshot of why I care so deeply about young people. Here is what this young lady wrote.

> Dear Rodney,
>
> As I write this letter I'm thinking about suicide. My life is in total confusion. I've tried everything but nothing seems to work. You came to my school and spoke, so I'm turning to you as my last hope. I don't want to die, but I don't think hell can be any worse than what I'm experiencing in my life at the moment.

> My parents don't realize what is happening to me
> because they don't care enough even to look. I
> thought drugs would be my way out, but really it's just
> been the path to more problems. I know I'm at a dead
> end. I'm scared and lonely. Rodney, is there any way
> you can please help me?

Many of us are naive about what's going on in the hearts of our kids. By the time a parent or grandparent discovers what's going on, it could be too late. Time and time again I hear from young people across the country who say, "I can't talk to my parents." "My parents are never home." "They just don't have the time to listen to me." "My parents just don't seem to care." "My parents just don't understand."

When parents hear such comments, they think to themselves, *I wonder if these kids really mean what they say?* After speaking to tens of thousands of young people, I've come to realize the perception of many young people is that their parents just don't care about them.

On the flip side of that coin, I hear from parents who tell me, "Rodney, I can't talk to my kids." "Everything I try to do or everything I try to say just seems to go through one ear and out the other." "Our kids have a mind of their own." "There's a bad attitude we can't seem to get a handle on in our home." Obviously, many of us see a widening gap of communication between parents and kids. Serious breakdowns in communication result in frustration, disappointment, and hurt.

This communication problem reminds me of the woman who went to talk to her lawyer about divorcing her husband. She walked into her lawyer's office one afternoon and said, "I want to divorce my husband."

Her lawyer perked up and said, "What's the problem?"

The woman started rambling, so the lawyer interrupted her, "No, be specific and tell me what's the problem?"

She asked, "What do you mean?"

He answered, "Well, do you have any grounds?"

She replied, "Yes, we have about forty acres up there in the north end of town."

He laughed, "Come on, lady. That's not what I'm talking about. Do you have a grudge?"

She said, "No, but we have a nice carport on the side of our house."

He said, "Come on, ma'am. We need to make this personal."

She asked, "What do you mean?"

He explained, "For example, does that man ever beat you up?"

She said, "Of course not. I'm up every morning about an hour to an hour and a half before he even turns over."

About this time the lawyer was getting a little frustrated, so he asked the lady, "Ma'am, would you be perfectly honest with me? Do you take any personal responsibility for the problems in your marriage?"

She wondered out loud, "What do you mean?"

He explained to her, "For example, do you ever wake up grouchy?"

She said, "Are you kidding? I just let him lay there. He gets up whenever he's ready."

The lawyer had taken all he could take. He looked at the lady and said, "Ma'am, why do you want to divorce your husband?"

The woman looked him in the eye and said, "I'm here to tell you the man can't seem to communicate."

This silly example illustrates what often happens between parents and their kids. They can't seem to communicate, especially when it comes to seeing eye to eye on the difficult issues that create conflict in the home. Young people long for rich, real communication with their parents. In order to let down their defenses, kids need six basic assurances from their parents. The first and fundamental thing they long for is forgiveness.

They Long for Forgiveness

Young people long to experience genuine forgiveness—not excuses or denials, but the real thing. Ephesians 4:32 tells us: "And be kind to one another, tenderhearted, forgiving one another, even as God in Christ forgave you" (RSV). The great Christian leader Charles Spurgeon once said, "Let us go to Calvary so that we may learn how to be forgiven, and then let's linger there so that we may know how to forgive." A lot of young people haven't spoken to their parents in years because someone was deeply offended. Because of that offense, a grudge destroyed the relationship. I've talked to parents who haven't spoken to their child in years because of painful things that were said or done, an embarrassing lifestyle that was lived, or shame that was brought upon the family. Their child was cut off and pushed to the side, an outcast who was no longer accepted.

This cycle of pain and bitterness happens in many of our homes, even Christian ones. It breaks my heart, but I can't imagine how it breaks the heart of God to see how bitterness destroys so many of our families. Young people today are going to make mistakes—just as we did. There is no perfect kid. We've all sinned; there is none righteous. Young people say things to their parents that cut like a knife. Many parents take it personally and become deeply offended by what they hear. Tragically, many of them refuse to forgive. The bitterness grows; the gap in the relationship widens.

You may spend sleepless nights because of the things your kids say or do. You experience times of frustration, disappointment, and embarrassment, but your relationship with your son or daughter is founded on the fundamental willingness to forgive and move beyond the offenses. If you allow an unforgiving spirit to take root in your heart, it will soon turn to resentment. Resentment then colors every conversation and every action with your teenager. And resentment then turns to an entrenched, ugly, destructive sense of bitterness.

Bitterness eats away at us. It causes self-destruction spiritually, mentally, emotionally, and even physically. I believe with all my heart that the greatest single enemy that is destroying our marriages and families is an unforgiving spirit.

A classic example of the way parents ought to respond to children who have embarrassed them or fallen short of their expectations is found in Luke 15, the story of the prodigal son. One son was a renegade; the other was faithful and obedient to his father's wishes. The younger son demanded that his father advance his inheritance. The father conceded, and the young man took the money and went to a far country. He wanted to be free from his father's expectations and free from the demands of home. He wanted to be free from rules and regulations.

Many young people today want the freedom to do their own thing. I meet young people who believe: "If no one else cares, then why should I care." They live for the moment. They've become thrill seekers. But the Bible says we reap what we sow. If a young person wants freedom, he has to earn that freedom. Kids say, "I just wish my parents would trust me more." But trust has to be earned.

The prodigal son lived it up and did what he longed to do. Eventually he ran out of money, and he soon ran out of friends. He finally hit rock bottom emotionally, spiritually, and morally. The Bible says, "He came to his senses" (v. 17). He woke up and found himself, a Jewish man, in the middle of a pig pen! He remembered the way life used to be back with his father. Suddenly things didn't seem so bad at home after all. He stood up in the pig pen and said, "I'm going back to my father's house, and I'm going to tell my dad I've sinned against him and sinned against God." And he headed down the road toward home.

Since the day his son left home, the father had been praying and believing that one day his son would return. Through the long months, he kept praying, persistent and faithful. He trusted that someday, somehow, God would intervene. Some parents reading this book are in that same place right now. You've done all you can do, and now all you can do is pray. You have to let go and let God take over. That's what the prodigal's father did, and God answered his prayer. One day (we don't know how many months or years the son was away, but it was probably a long time), the father looked down the road and saw his son as a dot in the distance. He strained his eyes to be sure, and after a few minutes he realized it was true! His son was coming home! The father ran down the road and threw his arms around his boy.

The son looked at his dad and said, "Father, I've sinned against you, and I've sinned against God." As the father looked at his son, he was still dealing with all the emotions of the last months and years—hurt, pain, rejection, disappointment, humiliation, embarrassment. All these feelings were just as real to him as they are to you. But he chose to forgive. He embraced his son and welcomed him back with no word of condemnation.

In his excellent book *The Freedom of Forgiveness,* David Augsburger outlines a four-step process to help us forgive and clear up the complexion of our relationships. He suggests:

1. *Forgive immediately.* When others hurt us, we naturally dwell on thoughts of self-pity and revenge. Recognize these thoughts and identify them as destructive to you and to your relationship with your teenager. As soon as you feel the pain of any offense, choose to forgive. Be honest about how much it hurts, but don't wait until you *feel* like forgiving. That day may never come! Choose to forgive even when you don't feel like it, even when you want to hurt the one who hurt you. Forgiveness is a choice, not an emotion.

2. *Forgive continually.* Forgiveness is unilateral; that is, we do it whether the other person is sorry or not, whether he changes or not, or whether it will happen again or not. People who love well are good forgivers. Learn to forgive as often and as deeply as offenses occur. Don't let them stack up. If they do, we become preoccupied with our hurt, and our thoughts drift toward getting even. Forgive the big offenses as well as the little annoyances. Don't let anything get in the way of a wonderful, loving relationship.

3. *Forgive and forget.* No, you don't get a lobotomy when you forgive, but you do choose to avoid dwelling on the offense. Don't become absorbed in the "if onlys" and "what ifs" of life. Don't give the wounds of the past the power to shape your future. Choose to think about the positives in the other person, and focus on hope, not hurt.

4. *Forgive and be healed.* When we forgive, we are admitting that something hurt us, and hurts need to be healed. Allow the grace of God to penetrate deeply into your heart. Many parents are devastated by the things their kids have done. Something dear to them—their hopes for their kids—has been damaged. In some cases, the direction of the young person's life is altered by drug addiction, a careless and tragic accident, or an unwanted pregnancy. These are losses almost as severe as a death in the family, and losses need to be grieved. When we allow ourselves to feel the pain, we invite God to touch us at our heart's deepest level. That's where genuine healing occurs. After a while, we again find that God is good and sovereign, and we find hope in the future.[1]

I've talked to young people all over this nation who would give anything to be reconciled with their parents, and I've talked to parents who would give anything to be reconciled with their kids. They long for healing in their relationship. Young people long to be back home in the arms of Mom and Dad, but they're convinced that Mom or Dad would never forgive them, never let them live it down, never accept them. Do you know what young people want from Mom and Dad? They want forgiveness—unconditionally, with no strings attached.

They Long for Honesty

James wrote, "Confess your sins to each other and pray for each other so that you may be healed" (James 5:16). In our homes today, we need spiritual and emotional healing. Many parents feel terribly guilty because they're trying to be something they are not. Whether parents realize it or not, their kids can see right through them. Teenagers know whether or not their parents are real. They see all the inconsistencies, hypocrisies, and double standards. Rather than trying to push their sins under the rug and pretend they don't exist, parents need to be honest. They need to get real about their faults and failures, and be willing to confess their sins to their kids.

Little children put their parents on a pedestal—Supermom and Superdad can do no wrong. But when those little children grow up to be preteens and teenagers, they get a little wiser and more observant. They realize their parents are not quite as super as they thought. They see the mistakes, the sins, and the inconsistencies, and they long to hear six important words from their parents: "I admit I made a mistake."

Parents shouldn't be too prideful to look their kid in the eye and say, "I was wrong." "I made a bad decision." "I was wrong in the way I talked to you." "I was wrong in the way I acted out toward you." A lack of honesty creates a wall that parents can't seem to penetrate. They wonder why they can't seem to get through and enter into their kids' world, but the lack of integrity and honesty has created a barrier in the relationship. Young people are longing for their parents to confess their faults.

It's been said that the greatest single ingredient in every human relationship is the need for intimacy. Young people long to have openness, transparency, and vulnerability in the home so they can trust their parents. Josh McDowell says: "You can fool a fool, and you can con a con, but you can't kid a kid."[2] Now more than ever, we need to pray for each other and to encourage one another when we've hurt one another. The saying "Families that pray together stay together" is true. Families need to get on their knees before God and before one another and seek God, to ask him to forgive us when we fail and to change us to make us more loving, kind, and wise.

They Long for Love

A sixteen-year-old girl recently said to me, "Rodney, not once has my father ever told me the words 'I love you.'" And I often hear statements like this: "My father never puts his arms around me or tells me he loves me." In too many cases, this generation of youth is being raised without fathers, and these young people are in search of their fathers' love. Men, don't buy into the myth that showing love and affection to your kids is not "manly." That is a lie from the pit of hell. Young people yearn for the security that comes from a father's love. They desperately need their dads to demonstrate that love physically, verbally, and consistently to their kids.

Mothers, the single greatest thing you can do for your kids is to love your husband. Fathers, the single greatest thing you can do for your kids is to love your wife. When your children see love modeled in your marriage, they will feel more secure. That love will also filter down and overflow into your relationship with your kids. Paul tells us in 1 Corinthians 13:4–7, "Love is patient, love is kind. It does not envy, it does not boast, it is not proud. It is not rude, it is not self-seeking, it is not easily angered, it keeps no record of wrongs. Love does not delight in evil but rejoices with the truth. It always protects, always trusts, always hopes, always perseveres." That's the way God loves us, and that's the kind of love he wants us to have for each other—especially in our families.

Psychologists tell us that the human touch builds confidence and security. Young people long for that kind of confidence and security, knowing that Mom and Dad love them no matter what. Tonight before you go to bed, walk into your kid's room without saying a word (make sure you knock before you walk in because you never know what you're walking into), and put your arms around him and embrace him. Then whisper the words "I love you." Your kid may go into cardiac arrest or try to figure out if you're on drugs, but he'll love it. When he puts his head down on his pillow, he'll go to bed having more confidence and security, knowing that his parent loves him more than anything in the world.

Don't assume your kids know how much you love them. Affirm it and reaffirm it. Let them know. Demonstrate it often. God demonstrated that kind of love to us. Jesus Christ came into this world to bear our sins upon a cross—to be crucified, to be buried, to be raised up from the dead. Why? So that we could experience his forgiveness and have hope, meaning, purpose, and joy. God demonstrated his love for us by giving sacrificially and demonstratively. Parents need to do the same for their kids.

If you have trouble communicating that kind of love to your teenager, don't despair. You can't just manufacture it by yourself. It is produced by the Holy Spirit as we trust him to help us experience and express the love of God. When we receive Christ as Lord and Savior and experience his forgiveness, we become reconnected with the Father, who longs to embrace us, accept us, and forgive us. As we experience the Father's love, we can share that love with others, including our families.

They Long for Stability

The lack of security and stability that many young people feel is often rooted in a generalized, foreboding sense of doom. Depression is now the second-leading illness in the public school campus next to the common cold. One out of every three teenagers in America has suicidal tendencies; one out of every six actually makes the suicide attempt.[3] It is no wonder that many of our kids today are growing up with emotional instability.

Years ago Dr. Armand Nicholi a Harvard professor said, "If one factor influences the character development and emotional stability of a person, it is the quality of the relationship he experiences as a child with both of his parents."[4] An amazing number of young people today are growing up with an emotional and spiritual vacuum in their lives. Many parents ask me the question, "What can we do? How can we build stability in the lives of our kids?"

In Matthew 7:24–25, Jesus said, "Therefore whoever hears these sayings of Mine, and does them, I will liken him to a wise man who built his house on the rock: and the rain descended, the floods came, and the winds blew and beat on that house; and it did not fall, for it was founded on the rock" (NKJV). When the winds of temptation blow and the waves of stress beat upon the hearts of our kids, they need a firm foundation that is solid as a rock.

Parents can do three things to provide that firm foundation in the lives of their kids:

- They can build spiritual stability.
- They can build emotional stability.
- They can build moral stability.

Young people today are obviously struggling with spiritual instability. We live in a day when many young people no longer can discern the difference between right and wrong. A few years ago, I watched television coverage of the memorial services in Jonesboro, Arkansas, where an eleven-year-old and a thirteen-year-old had gunned down five innocent people—four children and one schoolteacher. As in many cases of this kind of violence, the perpetrators expressed little or no remorse. They appeared to lack a moral compass. Having no discernment to make wise decisions, they seemed to fear no consequences.

The present generation of youth is reaping what previous generations have sown. When you take God, the Bible, and prayer out of the classroom and replace it with secular humanism, students fail to learn absolutes. Consequently, they lose the sense of right and wrong. Many young people today don't know who they are, what they believe, or why they believe it. This is where parents can step in. God has called you as parents to build spiritual stability into the lives of your kids. Young people need to be taught that they are fearfully and wonderfully made, that they are in fact created in the very image of God. Young people need a clear understanding of who they are in the eyes of God. Their identity is not based on what they've done or not done, or how they succeeded or failed. Their identity is based on who they are in Christ—children of God who are loved and accepted unconditionally.

Parents, you must learn to model spiritual, emotional, and moral stability in the home. Your kids' standards determine their values, and their values determine their judgments. Their judgments determine their choices, and their choices determine their decisions. Their decisions determine their character, and their character ultimately determines their greatness or failure in life. Parents have the unspeakable responsibility and privilege to build spiritual, emotional and moral stability into the lives of their children. Young people crave that kind of stability.

They Long for Attention

A little girl was asked by her third-grade teacher, "Who is your favorite person in the world?"

The little third-grader spoke up and said confidently, "My grandmother."

The teacher asked, "Your grandmother? Why?"

The little girl couldn't quite put into words how she felt about her grandmother, so she took out a piece of paper and a crayon and wrote out something that she titled "What's a Grandmother?" Here's what she wrote:

> A grandmother is a lady who has no children of
> her own. She likes other people's little girls and boys.
> A grandfather is a man grandmother. He goes for
> walks with the boys and talks about fishing and stuff
> like that. Grandmothers don't have to do anything

except be there. They're old so they shouldn't have to play hard or run. It's enough that they drive us to the market where the pretend horses are, and they have lots of dimes ready. Or if they take us for walks, they should slow down past things like pretty leaves and caterpillars. They should never say, "Hurry up." Usually grandmothers are fat, but not too fat to tie your shoes. They wear glasses and funny underwear. They can take their teeth and gums off. Grandmothers don't have to be smart, only answer questions like, Why isn't God married? How come dogs chase cats? Grandmothers don't talk baby talk like visitors do because it's too hard to understand. When they read to us, they don't skip or mind if it's the same story over and over again. Everybody should try to have a grandmother, especially if you don't have a television, because they are the only grown-ups who have time.[5]

Parents today are busier than ever. They don't spend much time with their kids, so they give them plenty of money to occupy them (and relieve their own guilt). Because many families have both parents making salaries, many of these families struggle trying to juggle the demands of home as well as work. They long to give time and attention to their children, but they are overwhelmed by the responsibilities of their careers. Since they don't feel that they can give as much time as they like, some of them strive to become even more successful so they can buy nice things, hoping that all the material things will be an outward expression of their love. They end up spelling love: M-O-N-E-Y.

I've met young people all over America who drive new cars and wear the latest styles of clothing, but they're also addicted to alcohol, strung out on cocaine, or living a promiscuous lifestyle. Many more are simply alone, lost, and empty. They have everything anybody could want—except love. I ask these young people, "If you have everything life has to offer, what made you choose this lifestyle?"

Many times, tears flow down their faces when they tell me, "I'd be willing to give up all those nice things my parents worked so hard to get if my parents would just take the time to stop, look, and listen—to notice that I even exist."

You ought to spell out love to your kids: T-I-M-E. Whatever you do, make time with your family a priority. Make it a priority in your marriage. Make it a priority in the relationships with your kids. You must be there for your kids when it really matters the most. Young people crave your attention.

They Long for Fairness

Colossians 3:21 states, "Fathers, provoke not your children to anger, lest they be discouraged" (KJV). Time and time again I hear from young people across the country, "I can't seem to please my parents. No matter what I do or how well I do it, it's never enough. I can't seem to live up to their expectations. I can't live up to their standards." Many parents put unrealistic expectations on their kids. Unfortunately, many parents are guilty of trying to live out their own dreams through the lives of their kids, so they push their kids to attain goals they always wanted to achieve. Many kids have become emotionally burned out because their parents pushed them to higher and higher levels in grades or athletics.

Don't misunderstand me. I believe parents should challenge their young people to strive for excellence in everything they do but not at the expense of their self-worth. When a young person begins to put his identity in his grades, he soon believes he's only as good as his grades. When young people are taught that winning is everything, they soon believe: "I'm only as good as my accomplishments. I'm only as good as my performance or the trophies I have in my cabinet." Young people need to know they're unconditionally loved and accepted, not only in the eyes of God, but in the eyes of Mom and Dad. No strings attached.

Expect the best from your kids, but don't demand perfection from them. Young people long to be treated fairly. The greatest single thing parents can do is to communicate the following five simple words: "You did a great job!" Be your kid's number one fan. Be his constant support—spiritually, emotionally, and morally. Be there for your kids when it really matters the most.

A Closer Look

1. Evaluate the extent your teenager's needs are being met. Chart it on a scale of 0 (not at all) to 10 (all day, every day):

    - Forgiveness
    0————————————5————————————10

    - Honesty
    0————————————5————————————10

    - Love
    0————————————5————————————10

    - Stability
    0————————————5————————————10

    - Attention
    0————————————5————————————10

    - Fairness
    0————————————5————————————10

2. What does this evaluation tell you about your teenager's needs?

3. What areas do you need to focus on to meet your teenager's needs? How will you take steps in that direction?

ELEVEN

CREATING AN ATMOSPHERE OF PEACE

Young people today are looking for peace at home. This generation is being raised in a society where divorce and remarriage are quite common. If young people aren't from a broken home themselves, many of their friends are. Yet the stress of life goes far beyond broken homes. Kids worry about violence, gangs, and disease. As they watch the news or check the Internet, the evidence of war, terrorism, and evil are now closer to home adding to the great need for peace our teenagers feel.

OBSTACLES TO PEACE

The only way we can have genuine and lasting peace is to know Christ as Lord and Savior. We need to make him the center of our lives as well as the center of our homes. Let's look at some of the obstacles to peace.

Pressure

Now more than ever, young people are faced with enormous pressures. Divorce is a common experience for parents, and the kids suffer too. Many young people are forced to choose to live with either Mom or Dad. If they choose to live with Dad, their mom feels angry and jealous. If they choose to live with Mom, Dad often feels bitter. In addition, blended families add the pressure of trying to adjust to a new stepmom or stepdad or stepbrothers and stepsisters. The family dynamics can be incredibly confusing and complicated.

Young people also experience tremendous peer pressure to use drugs, get involved in premarital sex, drink alcohol, run with the gangs, dabble in the occult, and conform to the world's ideals of beauty, wealth, and strength. Unfortunately, many kids give in to these pressures. They desperately want to fit in and have a sense of belonging, so they are tempted to try anything to be accepted.

Escape

Many young people are looking for a way out, an escape from all the problems at home and pressures at school. They may try to isolate themselves from pain by taking drugs or by being a loner. Some try to end the pain by suicide. Most attempt to get away from the pressures by filling their lives with enough distractions to dull the pain.

Availability

In our society, all kinds of things—both good and bad—are readily available to young people. Technology has brought the world to our fingertips, and wealth has given us incredible opportunities to fulfill our dreams. The flip side is that we are plagued with sins and diseases unheard of only a few years ago. AIDS is an epidemic in Africa and in some cities in America. The teen pregnancy rate is astronomical. Who would have ever imagined we'd have condom distribution on many of our school campuses across the nation?

Who would have ever imagined that alcohol and drugs would run rampant in our schools—during classes? And who would have imagined illegal weapons would be brought to school?

Curiosity

Young people want to experiment with almost everything. Most of them want to know what it's like to get high. By the end of high school, two-thirds of American teenagers have used illicit drugs.[1] The media actually encourages this behavior. The average young person watches more than one hundred thousand alcohol-related television commercials before reaching the legal drinking age.[2] It is no wonder that 30 percent of our nation's nine-year-olds now admit they are tempted to drink.[3]

According to the National Council on Alcoholism, more than one hundred thousand ten- and eleven-year-olds report getting drunk at least once a week. When I go to public school campuses across the country, most principals tell me alcohol is the most significant problem they face. Kids see Mom and Dad drinking, and because they also see the role models on television drinking they feel justified in drinking too. But when kids drink, they don't just drink to be sociable—they get drunk. One out of every nine high school students in America is considered to be a binge drinker.[4] They believe drinking is a way to be accepted and have an identity. They also see drinking as a way of escaping their problems and numbing the pain. Unfortunately, it only amplifies their problems and pain.

Kids are curious about sex. In the next twelve months, the average young person will watch nearly ten thousand sexual scenes on television. Out of those scenes, more than 81 percent depict sex outside marriage.[5] Hollywood paints the picture that it's fine to have sex and not worry about the consequences. Because of the unquenchable desire kids have to love and be loved, they want to experience sexual intimacy. When a young man and young woman give up their virginity hoping to find love, acceptance, and approval, invariably they get hurt—experiencing rejection, humiliation, and confusion instead.

Emptiness

Our teens' desperate search for peace too often ends in deeper and more painful emptiness. I was at the Atlanta airport recently changing planes. I had a long layover, so I went to a newsstand to buy a newspaper. Near the checkout register I saw a magazine with a cover picture of Marilyn Manson. Under the photograph was the title of an article about today's youth. I picked it up and thumbed through it, and I saw a statement that said, "Today's generation of youth are coming of age, but they're already spent." In other words, once young men and women graduate from high school, they've already "been there, done that." They've tried everything there is to try, but they're still left disillusioned, dissatisfied, and empty. These are seventeen- or eighteen-year-old kids who, at the very moment they ought to be experiencing life at it's fullest, find life no longer worth living. That's the reason nineteen kids a day commit suicide—their lives are empty and shattered.

This is true not only for the kids in the ghetto but for many of the young people living under our own roofs. Christian parents often tell me, "I understand this is a reality in the world, but we are a Christian family, and our kids are in Christian schools. We try to instill Christian values in our kids, so this news is irrelevant to us." Not so! Christian young people experience the same pitfalls as other youth. A few years ago, Barna Research Group conducted a national survey of nearly four thousand Christian youth. They discovered that 57 percent of America's church-going youth can no longer affirm that an objective standard for right and wrong exists.[6] In other words, there's not much difference in Christian kids' values, lifestyles, and behaviors compared to unbelievers. This reality concerns me and weighs heavily upon my heart. I believe it breaks the heart of God. I believe Christian parents need all the help and hope they can get to help their kids avoid making the wrong choices and falling into the same traps and pitfalls that so many other kids fall into.

Creating a New Atmosphere

Some of us need to do a hard-nosed analysis of what's going on in our families—and in our own lives. If we are courageous enough to be honest, we will have the willpower to make changes that can radically affect each family member for good. Creating a new atmosphere in our homes doesn't happen by accident, and it doesn't happen by just wishing it would take place. No, we have to have a clear plan and take action. It's never too late to start doing what is right. I believe God can enable us to establish new habits and make a fresh commitment to start over and build a family focused on God and his ways. As children of God, we have everything we need to help our children find direction, fulfillment, and everlasting peace.

The greatest influence on a young person's life is his parents, not his peers. The time and energy spent raising children is the most important investment we'll ever make, far more than any investment we'll make in our company or occupation. I hear about companies spending millions of dollars on consulting fees to learn how to grow the business. If they can spend millions to restructure or reorganize to ensure success for the future of their company, why can't we invest our time and energies in our children? We have the responsibility and the privilege to raise the next generation of men and women whom God may use to bring spiritual awakening to our nation. To build them into strong, godly people, we need to create a new atmosphere of love, affirmation, and peace.

Deuteronomy 6:5 is the single most important commandment given in the entire Word of God. It instructs us, "Love the Lord your God with all your heart and with all your soul and with all your strength." If we are honest, we must admit that there have been many times when we have chosen to do our thing rather than God's will. We continually need to remember that Christ is the single most important thing in our lives—our focus, the hub of our wheel.

If Jesus is not the Lord in our personal lives, Jesus is not going to be the Lord in our marriages. If Jesus Christ is not Lord in our marriages, Jesus is not going to be Lord in our homes. If Jesus isn't Lord in our homes, we can't expect Jesus to be Lord in the lives of our kids. Modeling the message in our homes is absolutely necessary. Deuteronomy 6:6–9 also instructs us to allow the Ten Commandments to be written upon our hearts so we can impress them on our children. We need to talk about them when we sit at home, when we walk along the road, when we lie down, and when we get up. Speaking to the Jewish custom of the time, the instruction is to tie them as symbols on our hands and bind them on our foreheads, write them on the doorframes of our houses and upon our gates. As we are absorbed in the life of Christ, his presence and his Spirit will pervade our homes, and we will be empowered and strengthened by the power of the Holy Spirit.

It's been said that parenting is simple—it's just not easy. Each of us needs all the help we can get. God has given us the greatest blueprint of all to follow. He has given us guidelines and instructions in his Word. We can create an atmosphere of peace if we follow his directions. I've learned these guidelines as I've read the Scriptures and as I've interacted with successful parents. I've interviewed and studied these parents, asking them to tell me their secrets. I've also asked their kids to tell me what their parents did that was so influential in their lives. The following principles are ones they shared with me.

A Good Parent Is Accessible.

James Dobson, founder and president of Focus on the Family, tells us the average parents spend less than fourteen minutes a week engaged in meaningful conversation with their kids. Some of us are so busy that we no longer have time for the people who matter the most. I'm from the big city of Dallas, so I haven't done much hunting and fishing. The few experiences I've had of hunting have been a complete disaster. I'm not one of these guys who wants to get up at four in the morning (before God wakes up) to go out in the bushes or on the lake, but I've been told by successful fisherman that if you're going to go catch fish, you don't go when it's convenient for you. You don't go at two in the afternoon and expect to load up the boat with fish. You have to go early in the morning or late at night. In order to be successful, you have to go when the fish are biting.

The same principle is true concerning entering the world of young people. You're not going to have an open, vulnerable, transparent, intimate relationship with your kids when it's convenient for you. They may want to talk at 2:00 A.M. or just minutes before they walk out the door to go to school. Whatever you do as parents, make yourself available to be there for your kids when it really matters the most to *them*. Open the door of communication. Kids need to see you as someone they can trust, someone who won't betray them, someone who won't slam them, and someone who will really listen to what's going on in their lives. You may not like what you hear, but listen anyway. Many kids feel they can't talk to their parents. Because past attempts were negative, they got the impression that Mom and Dad just don't care to understand. Set aside at least one night a week to hang out as a family and have a good time. Do something creative, and make yourselves available. Create memories that your kids will always treasure.

A Good Parent Is Discerning.

Parents can get so busy that they lose sight of what's going on in their kids' world. We can assume everything is going along fine when, in reality, disaster is lurking around the next corner. We need to be alert and observant because, as Jesus warned us, "Satan has come to steal, kill and destroy" (John 10:10 NIV, paraphrased). Satan, the enemy, will do everything he can to lure your kids into compromising, destructive situations. He'll tempt them, coerce them, and drive them into a vulnerable situation where they feel trapped. Then he's got them.

I know some Christian parents who put their kids in Christian schools to isolate them from the dangers of the world. They think this protection will help their kids make the right choices. They relax and trust the school to parent their children. After all, their kids go to church and are involved in youth groups; what could possibly go wrong? These passive, naive parents are actually neglecting their responsibility—trusting someone else to do what God has called *them* to do.

Many parents tell me that they know teenage destructive behavior is "out there," but they say, "We have an open relationship with our daughter. She would never do these kind of things." It's been said that when an ostrich buries its head in the sand to avoid unpleasant facts, it not only represents an undignified spectacle, it also constitutes an irresistible target. Don't put your head in the sand so that you don't have a clue what's going on in your home.

Parents need to be alert. Don't get so busy and preoccupied with what's going on in your world that you lose sight of what's going on in the world of your kids. Take notice of the subtle signs and the obvious symptoms that your kids display. Stop, look, and listen. Be discerning.

A Good Parent Shows Affection.

Studies reveal a significant decline in parents' verbal and physical affection as children enter the teenage years. For instance, 68 percent of mothers give hugs, kisses, and pats to their fifth graders, but only 44 percent physically pamper their ninth graders. Fifty percent of fathers show physical affection to fifth graders as opposed to 26 percent to ninth graders. The statistics drop even further for older teenagers.[7] At the very time kids need more love, affection, approval, and attention, they receive it less and less from the most important people in their lives.

Many kids confide in me, quite often with tears flowing down their faces. They say, "No one has ever told me they love me. My parents have never communicated that to me." In fact, many parents and adults across the country say they can relate to that sentiment in regards to their own parents. They have never heard the words "I love you" from their father; they can't remember Dad putting his arms around them or Mom affirming her love to them. Now is the time to fill this void. Demonstrate to your kids physically and verbally how much you care. Don't assume they already know how much you love them. They need to be reminded again and again.

A Good Parent Is Wise.

A number of years ago I heard Zig Ziglar tell a story about Andrew Carnegie; one of the most successful businessmen in America. He came from his native land of Scotland with nothing to his name, but through business genius he went from rags to riches. In fact, he became one of the largest steel manufacturers in America. At one time Carnegie had forty-three millionaires working for him. A local reporter was intrigued by his success story and wanted to learn his secret of success. He asked Mr. Carnegie, "I understand you have forty-three millionaires working for you; is that true?"

Mr. Carnegie told him, "Yes, that's true, but you need to understand, none of those men were millionaires before they came to work for me. They've all become millionaires as a result of working for me."

The reporter said, "That's why I came to interview you. What's the secret of your success? What was it about these men that you thought was so great that you were willing to invest everything that you have in them?"

Carnegie replied, "Sir, you need to understand something. Investing in people, developing people, is kind of like mining for gold. When a person goes into the gold mine to mine for gold, the very first thing that has to happen is several tons of dirt must be removed in order to find a single ounce of gold. But when a person first goes into the gold mine, he isn't looking for the dirt. He's looking for the gold."

I believe wise parents look beyond the dirt, beyond the flaws, and beyond the failures and blemishes in their imperfect kids. Rather than reminding their kids what failures they are, wise parents are able to find the gold. They're able to pull out those abilities, talents, and gifts that God has given their kids. They're able to nurture those gifts and talents. Wise parents help their kids rise above their circumstances and failures. They help their kids reach their true God-given potential.

As adults, many of us have stopped growing spiritually, mentally, emotionally, and physically. When we stop growing, our kids stop growing, too, because we model the message. You and I have an incredible challenge to model that message and to grow so our kids will see the value of stretching themselves to be all God wants them to be.

Wise parents establish good habits in their homes. Take your kids on a mission trip or minister to the homeless. Let your kids see you as a hands-on parent, and they'll follow your example.

A Good Parent Is Gracious.

My good friend Zig Ziglar says, "The average child has heard the words 'no' or 'you can't do that' at least 150,000 times by the time they reach the age of eighteen."[8] Isn't it amazing how easy it is to find ourselves tearing someone else down in order to build ourselves up? I heard a story about a little boy who got in a fight with his mom. He was so angry at his mom that he snarled, "I hate you! I hate you!" The little boy stormed out the door and went to the side of his house. On the side of the house was a large valley. The little boy yelled out, "I hate you! I hate you!" As he hollered those words out, those words came back. The boy heard his echo. He was so scared that he ran back inside the house and told his mom, "There's a mean boy on the other side of the valley who said he hates me!"

The wise mom took her son to the side of the house. On the hillside she said, "Son, I want you to yell as loud as you can the words 'I love you.'"

That little boy reared back and hollered as loud as he could, "I love you!" Before he knew it, the words echoed back.

Life is an echo. What you send out comes back. What you sow you reap. What you see in others exists in you. Ephesians 4:29 says, "Do not let any unwholesome talk come out of your mouths, but only what is helpful for building others up according to their needs, that it may benefit those who listen." The way you see your kids and the way you treat them is the way they often become.

As I was on my way from Chicago to Columbus, I observed some parents yelling at their kids, "Sit down! Don't do that, you moron!" Throughout the plane flight, these parents constantly berated their kids. What do you think these kids will start believing about themselves? When prison inmates across America were asked what they were told as kids, many of them said they were told, "They'll put you in jail for doing that!" They soon believed what they were told, and the threat became a reality.

Be kind to your kids. Make sure what comes out of your mouth builds them up instead of tears them down. Say things to your kids that you won't regret later. You can never take those words back. The old saying "Sticks and stones may break my bones, but words can never hurt me" is a lie. Words can cut like a knife. A lot of our kids are walking around wounded because all they ever hear are cutting, destructive, venomous remarks from Mom and Dad, and they never get over it.

A Good Parent Models the Message.

According to a study conducted in Missouri, 60–65 percent of a person's vocabulary is acquired by the age of three, and two-thirds of everything he will ever know will have been learned by the age of six.[9] The first six years of children's lives are critical, foundational, and pivotal. That's why it is so important for parents to model that message and be an example. An old, familiar poem tells us a lot about the need to be consistent models for our children.

Children Live What They Learn

If a child lives with criticism, he learns to condemn.
If a child lives with hostility, he learns violence.
If a child lives with ridicule, he learns to be shy.
If a child lives with shame, he learns to feel guilty.
If a child lives with encouragement, he learns confidence.
If a child lives with praise, he learns to appreciate.
If a child lives with fairness, he learns justice.
If a child lives with security, he learns faith.
If a child lives with approval, he learns to like himself.
If a child lives with acceptance and friendship, he learns
   to love the world.[10]

In Luke 6:39–40, Jesus asks profound questions and gives us a clear insight: "Can a blind man lead a blind man? Will they not both fall into a pit? A student is not above his teacher, but everyone who is fully trained will be like his teacher." A modern-day translation of this passage is that kids live what they learn. They learn to live by watching you. Many kids confess to me that they've lost all respect for their parents because they exhibit a double standard: "My dad tells me to be good, but he's an alcoholic," or "My mom rags on me to stay away from sex, but she's having an affair." Kids see the hypocrisy and the inconsistency.

Many parents repeat the lie "Just do as I say, not as I do." Rules without a relationship lead to rebellion. A relationship with rules produces respect. Unfortunately, a lot of kids have lost respect for their parents because all they hear are dos and don'ts—regulations without a relationship. Their emotional needs aren't met. They've been neglected and ignored. Warmth, affirmation, and encouragement are as necessary to them as correction. Rules and relationship are like two wings of an airplane: both are absolutely necessary.

A Good Parent Is Strong and Honest.

According to a study taken by the Zero Population Growth Institute, it takes $150,000 to raise a child from infancy to the age of eighteen. However, it takes a lot more than money. It takes the wisdom of Solomon, the patience of Job, the strength of Sampson, the protection of a thousand guardian angels, and a ton of love.[11] It takes courage to be a parent. It takes courage for a parent to look their kids in the eye and tell them when they're wrong. It takes courage for parents to take a stand for what's right. It takes courage for parents to show up at school board meetings and speak out for their kids. It takes courage for parents to confront a teacher. It takes courage for parents to swallow their pride, humble themselves, and admit that their kid isn't perfect. It takes courage for parents to do what's right, even though they get no appreciation or gratitude in return. It takes courage for parents to do what's right, even though their son or daughter may rebel against them. It takes courage for a parent to admit their own faults, failures, and mistakes.

Your kids already know you're not perfect. From time to time they'd like to hear you admit it. Honesty takes strength and courage.

My Family's Story

I am an answer to a prayer. I'm the youngest of four boys in my family. My dad's name is Freddie Gage. For the last forty-five years my father has traveled all over America, and God has used him to reach more than a million people through his ministry as an evangelist. My father was born in Houston, Texas. He grew up in a dysfunctional home and his father was an alcoholic. My dad vitually raised himself with very little supervision. As a teenager, my dad started using drugs and became a street gang leader. My dad was seventeen when he married my mom on her fifteenth birthday. Living with him was so traumatic that my mom filed for divorce shortly after they got married. By the grace of God, my parents came to know Christ. He radically changed their lives and brought reconciliation and healing to their marriage.

My oldest brother, Daniel, was kicked out of the house when he was eighteen years old. He was told not to come back home until he got right with God. Daniel was using alcohol and drugs. At the age of twenty-four, Daniel gave his life to Christ. Today, Daniel is serving the Lord in full-time ministry.

My next-to-the-oldest brother, Paul, followed a similar path. Alcohol and drugs almost ruined him. He gave his life to Christ when he was nineteen years old, but it wasn't until he was twenty-four or twenty-five years of age that he really began to walk with God. Christ changed his life, and today my brother Paul is serving the Lord in full-time ministry.

My third brother, Rick, was an outstanding athlete who played college football. He wanted to be a major football coach, so after he graduated, he started coaching college football. He first went to West Texas State University, then after two years he went to Texas Tech University in Lubbock, Texas. He was twenty-five years old, single, and an assistant football coach at Texas Tech University. He traveled all over the country, living in the limelight in front of thousands of people. Rick soon got caught up in the lifestyle of fame and drugs. When he was twenty-five, an evangelist friend of ours named James Robison was holding a crusade in Lubbock. My dad called my brother and pleaded for him to go hear James preach. Rick went with the intention of showing up late and leaving early. Because Rick was a preacher's kid, his attitude was that he had heard them all and seen them all. But God had other plans for Rick that night. He went forward and gave his life to Christ. Today, my brother Rick is serving the Lord in full-time ministry preaching the gospel.

There's a seven-year difference between Rick and me. I often felt like an only child because my three older brothers were grown and out of the house when I was growing up. I wanted to be like my older brothers. I idolized them. I wanted to prove to my friends I could be just as cool as they were even though my dad was a preacher. I did some things I deeply regret because I wanted to fit in and have my own identity. It wasn't until I was eighteen years old that I gave my life to Christ. Praise God, Christ changed my life. I tell people all the time that I'm not what I want to be, and I'm not what I ought to be, but because of Jesus, I'm not what I used to be. Jesus changed my life.

My parents had four sons, and all four in some way became prodigals. Years ago in the middle of all the turmoil in our family, my parents would probably have said something very similar to what many of you would say today: "If we had it to do all over again, we'd probably do things differently." As their son, let me tell you what they did right. My parents were dependent on the Word of God. They didn't grow up with a Christian bookstore on every corner, and they didn't have many of the resources you and I have. All they had was the Word of God—but that's all they needed. They knew that there was one thing they could count on—God. Even though they made parenting mistakes, they stayed true to one commitment: they did everything they could do to instill the Word of God into our hearts, minds, and lives. They knew that when all else failed, they could still cling to God's promises and principles. They knew God's Word was sharper than any two-edged sword. They knew God's Word would never return void. They also knew that they would reap what they had sown. As children, we were taught about God and instructed in the Word of God. Since God created us with a free will to make our own choices, we chose to do what was right in our own eyes. Fortunately, through experiencing the consequences of our own rebellion, God's Word and the teachings from our parents brought all four of us back to genuine repentance and life-change.

No matter how bad things are for you right now, don't throw in the towel. Don't call it quits no matter how badly your children have hurt you, disappointed you, let you down, embarrassed you, or humiliated you. Be courageous. Greater is he that is in you than he that is in the world. All of us wrestle against principalities and powers of this world. We are fighting hard, yet the battle has already been won. Jesus conquered it two thousand years ago. We battle with the evil forces of this world, and our children are worth fighting for. God wants to use you and me to bring glory to him and to turn our world right side up.

I have three kids of my own. It's a challenge to raise them, but it's worth every minute. The greatest investment I'll ever have is in my wife and kids. I might be the only Bible they'll ever read. I might be the only church they'll ever attend. I might be the only Jesus my wife and kids ever see. That's why I need to model the message, and I've got to make the greatest investment I can make in their precious lives. God wants to use you and me to make a difference in the lives of our kids.

A Closer Look

1. List some specific difficulties your teenager has with these obstacles to peace:
   - Pressure:
   - Escape:
   - Availability (of drugs, guns, etc.):
   - Curiosity:
   - Emptiness:

2. Rate yourself on a scale of 0 (not even on the chart) to 10 (best in the universe) in establishing and modeling these principles:

   - A Good Parent Is Accessible.

   0———————————5———————————10

   - A Good Parent Is Discerning.

   0———————————5———————————10

   - A Good Parent Shows Affection.

   0———————————5———————————10

   - A Good Parent Is Wise.

   0———————————5———————————10

   - A Good Parent Is Gracious.

   0———————————5———————————10

   - A Good Parent Models the Message.

   0———————————5———————————10

   - A Good Parent Is Strong and Honest.

   0———————————5———————————10

3. As you reflect on this evaluation, what are some things you are doing well as a parent?

4. What are some areas where you need to improve?

5. Write a prayer about these things:
   - Heavenly Father, I feel . . .
   - Almighty God, I want . . .
   - Lord, I will . . .

TWELVE

LIVING IN HOPE

Jane's son Scott had been a good kid. In junior high he had done well academically and played football and baseball. One day as he was playing football, he broke his leg. The leg took a long time to mend, and Scott gradually lost interest in sports. Instead, he became interested in music and started playing the guitar. He played pretty well, so he joined a band, but the band included some kids who were smoking dope. Scott enjoyed these boys, and he wanted to fit in. He was determined to do whatever it took to be "one of the guys."

About three years later, when he was seventeen, Scott was doing cocaine. He had also dropped acid and had even experimented with heroine. To fund his habit, he needed money—lots of money—so he started gambling. He played pool at a pool hall downtown and lost hundreds of dollars. He needed to find some other way to get cash.

Late one night the police called at Jane's house. They had arrested Scott for breaking and entering a Wal-Mart at three in the morning. Jane drove down to the store where the police were holding Scott. As she looked into her son's eyes, Jane's heart broke. How did it get to that point? What happened in Scott's life? What happened to that family that caused such a breakdown?

Jane was from an abusive home. Her father was emotionally distant, and her mother was an enraged alcoholic who used to scream at Jane; then the next morning, she'd hug her. Jane grew up a terrified little girl and became a terrified woman. She married a strong but emotionally distant man who was preoccupied with his work as an insurance agent.

During those years while Scott was in high school, Jane suspected her son was doing some stuff that he shouldn't have been doing, but Scott's father said, "It's no big deal. Boys will be boys." Even when Scott came in late with his breath smelling of alcohol and his eyes bloodshot, his father refused to open his eyes to see the obvious signs of drug use. Scott's dad also tried to compensate for his own late hours by giving his son money, a car, and an expensive guitar and amps. When Scott first lost money gambling, he'd come back to his father and say he needed more money. Jane listened and knew what was going on, but she felt helpless to stop the descent into darkness. Her fears often exploded in rage and blame, then she retreated into shame for losing control of herself. Scott and his dad watched her lose it, then they'd shake their heads and move on with their "game."

Jane found out that Scott was dealing drugs. Her solution was to yell at him, and this time even his dad got upset. But yelling and blaming was the extent of their solution. Scott learned that if he could endure their tirades, nothing else would happen, and he could go back to dealing drugs. This young man kept doing whatever he wanted to do. No boundaries; no consequences. Reality and change were far too threatening to Jane and her husband. Jane was afraid not only of her son and her husband but of her own raw emotions of fear and anger.

When the police called that night, something in Jane snapped. She realized things had gotten too far out of line. She drove down to the store where the police were holding her son. When Scott came out of the police car, Jane looked at him and said, "Scott, tell the truth. Were you trying to steal from the store?"

Scott hesitated a minute and said, "Yes, I was." At that moment Jane knew something had to change. She thought it might already be too late, but she was going to try. She faced the fact that her son was a drug addict, that he was out of control. He was also a criminal. There was no disputing these facts. The question was what to do about them.

Jane took Scott to a counselor who recommended that he go to Narcotics Anonymous (NA) meetings every day for ninety days. Jane and her husband required that Scott get a job. They weren't going to give him any more money. Jane also decided to do something she had done sporadically before but now was committed to do—she decided to pray. More than ever before, she was desperate that God would work, not only in Scott's life, but in her own. As she, the counselor, and the Narcotics Anonymous meetings put pressure on Scott to face the reality of his life, the young man became enraged. He had been enraged before, but now he turned his anger on his mother, God, and everybody else. It was an incredibly difficult time for this out-of-control family.

For months they struggled. Jane had to talk very honestly with her husband about his role as part of the problem. To his great credit, he acknowledged that the way he treated their son had not been beneficial. He didn't go to support group meetings himself, but at least he acknowledged there was a problem, and he was willing to go along with the counselor's recommendations.

Over the course of several months, the tension in the family rose and fell almost daily, sometimes several times a day. They struggled with their long-repressed anger, fears, and animosity, and they expressed these feelings to one another. They learned to talk about real difficulties in their relationship and resolve them. This process certainly was not pretty. The years of repressed emotions for Scott and the decades of repressed emotions for Jane sometimes seeped out—but more often they exploded in violent rage. Jane realized very early in this process that she had to get help for herself. She found a counselor so she could address her own problems, her own background, her own needs, and her anger at her husband, her son, and herself. Over the course of months, she learned to face reality, to grieve her deep hurts, and to make new decisions about how she could respond to difficult moments.

Jane and her husband set very clear boundaries and consequences for Scott. They stuck by those boundaries, and he hated them. In fact, he hated his parents. But as he listened to other people at NA meetings and as he listened to the counselor, he realized he was on a path that was going to wreck his life. Gradually he changed. God worked in his life.

One of the turning points for Scott occurred following an angry moment when all seemed lost, hopeless, and out of control. After the angry exchange, Jane sat in the living room on the sofa. She asked Scott to come sit next to her. She held his hands and she prayed. She asked God to take control of their lives—and Scott wept. This wasn't the end of their problems, but it was the beginning of the end—a fresh start for Scott and his relationship with his mother. Jane invited God to play his role in their lives. Yes, God had been playing a role before that, and he played a role after that, but Jane's prayer was the moment when they acknowledged that God was there, God was sovereign, and God was good.

The next several months proved to be incredibly difficult, but gradually the family came to a greater realization of hope, and they developed better skills of communication. The boundaries Jane and her husband set and enforced made a tremendous difference. At first there was increased tension, but Scott eventually realized that he was not going to be set free to do whatever he wanted to do again. His parents now enforced consequences, and he had to abide by the rules. Through all this, the relationship between Jane and her husband also improved. They had many tense moments because she was more honest with him, but gradually they came to understand one another and appreciate each other even more.

This isn't a story with a happy ending—yet. This family is still in the middle of working out the kinks, learning new ways to think and act, and making decisions every day to respond in positive, productive ways instead of ruining themselves and each other. They are learning to live in hope.

When we are wrestling with a defiant or depressed teenager, it is easy to lose sight of our ultimate goal of loving and honoring God. Our minds and hearts are consumed with the pain, the manipulation, and the fears of what might happen. But even in our darkest moments, God is there, and he is willing and able to work powerfully to give us wisdom and strength. No, he doesn't force our teenagers to become good and godly. The Lord gives us the wisdom to offer them choices, and then it's up to them to make their decisions.

The apostle Paul experienced enormous pressures and difficulties, but he kept his vision and purpose clear. He wrote the Corinthians, "So we make it our goal to please him" (2 Cor. 5:9). We call God "Lord" and "Master." We are created by him, and we live for him. He certainly doesn't cause anyone (like our teenagers) to make dumb choices, but he is willing to use even the dumbest of choices for good if we trust him. Remember Rachel's story? Her parents certainly feared that all was lost, but they prayed and wept and pleaded with God to work in their daughter's life. It took a long time, but today they see the clear hand of God at work in this beautiful young mother. She is wiser and stronger in her faith than she ever was before. No, that path of premarital sex and domination by her boyfriend wasn't the best path in the world, but once it was chosen by Rachel, God was willing to use even that to bring grace and truth into her life. She trusted God, and he made something terrible into a pillar of strength that honors him and blesses others.

When we face trials, difficulties, and mistakes, we can interpret them either as roadblocks or as stepping stones. If we believe they are roadblocks, we wither into self-pity and despair or rage and bitterness—or both. Then the problems do indeed become roadblocks. But if we see the difficulties as stepping stones, we trust God to use anything and everything to build, strengthen, and deepen us. We trust there is light even when all we see is darkness; we trust that God has a way even when all we see are dead ends. It is in that faith that we grow strong.

Some of us have endured and are currently enduring incredible heartaches. Sons have wasted their lives on drugs; daughters have run off with young men we do not respect and who use our daughters for their own purposes. We are tempted to quit—to give up on God, on our kids, and on ourselves. My friend, don't quit. Look again to God and trust that he is near. He may have a very different lesson for you than you ever imagined. Open your heart to him and let his Word speak deep into the recesses of your heart.

The only person you can control is yourself. You can't be obedient for your teenager or your spouse. You can only be faithful and accountable for your own choices—what you think about, your attitude, and your actions. As you cultivate faithfulness to God, he has promised to work in you to give you hope. I think again of the passage in Romans 5: "We also rejoice in our sufferings, because we know that suffering produces perseverance; perseverance, character; and character, hope. And hope does not disappoint us, because God has poured out his love into our hearts by the Holy Spirit, whom he has given us" (vv. 3–5). It takes a lot of faith to "rejoice in our sufferings," but if our eyes are on the goodness and sovereignty of God and we trust that he is at work even in our deepest struggles, we can hang on and persevere.

One of the truths we have seen in these pages is that our own parenting has been shaped, for good or ill, by our parents. How we treat our kids may not be exactly the same, but it is a product of our own parents' attitudes and actions. Our task now is not to blame them; it is to create a new legacy for our children, grandchildren, and generations to come. As we have the courage to model honesty, trust, and maturity, our legacy will become one of building instead of tearing down, of love instead of bitterness, of kindness instead of criticism. Changing a legacy can't be accomplished all at once. We take it one step at a time, day after day, situation after situation. The cumulative effect is a mosaic of love for our families.

Do you remember the story of Nancy and Melissa in chapter 1? I want to tell you the rest of that story now. The situation looked hopeless. Melissa had run away from home with her boyfriend Cory. Nancy and her husband had tried to make their home a loving, positive experience for their daughter, but it seemed that everything they did backfired. Now she was gone. Nancy continued her story:

> We knew Melissa was with Cory, so we tried to figure out where they had gone. First, we went to his house, but no one was there. We called the police, and they suggested that we give them a picture. We took her picture down to the bus station, but nobody there recognized her.
>
> I don't remember the next few days very clearly. We were so upset. It seemed like somebody had died! Church people came to our home to comfort us and pray for us. Stewart and I cried together. Our daughter was gone, and we had no idea where she was. We were so fearful and hurt. I had tried to be such a good mother—an ideal Christian mother to my girls. To me, this was a night of failure as a mother! Everything I had tried to do came tumbling down.
>
> The police helped us a lot. We called all of Cory's family and friends, but none of them said they knew anything about where they were. Nobody was talking.

None of them said they had talked to him or knew where he was or anything. We found out that Cory had expressed that he wanted to have a better relationship with his mother in Tampa, so we called her, but she said she didn't know anything about where they were. The police felt as if she knew more than she was saying. We talked to her several times, and in one of the later conversations, the police told us to tell her that her son could be charged with crimes. Melissa was only fifteen years old. Stewart told Cory's mother that he was taking on tremendous responsibilities by running off with our daughter.

I don't know if she was lying from the beginning or if they just showed up at her house and then she covered for them, but at that point, she told Cory to call us to let us know where they were. Actually, he didn't call, but she did. Two or three days later, she called our house. My husband was really strong with Cory and put a scare in him about the responsibilities of taking care of Melissa. I think that got through to him.

They finally agreed to come back to Ohio to see us and get counseling. Melissa was willing to come back, but she was stubborn and determined that she was going to date Cory. At that point my heart began to change. I became very angry with her. I thought, "She's made her bed. She can sleep in it! She wants Cory. She can have him! She can find out what kind of man he is! She'll be sorry, and she'll wish she'd never met him!" I felt so much anger toward her now that I knew she was safe. She said she didn't want to live at home, and I thought, *That's fine! If she doesn't want to live with us, she can go live somewhere else. That's just fine with me!*

When she came back, she moved in with a counselor. All of us were in counseling. We worked hard at it, and we drew up some new guidelines for family living. Stewart and I didn't feel very comfortable with them. We felt stretched, but if this is what it took to get our daughter back and be a family again, we were willing to do it. Eventually, after several weeks or months, Melissa came back home. Slowly things began to get better. When we allowed her to date Cory with her eyes wide open, then their relationship fell apart. Then Melissa told her counselor about Cory hitting her. When we gave her permission to do what she so desperately wanted to do, she didn't want to do it anymore.

At this point Melissa wanted to get away from Cory, but he made it very difficult because he is so possessive. He followed her and threatened her. He said he would kill himself if she didn't come back to him. Things really came to a head during this time. Melissa decided to end the relationship, and Cory exploded! Finally, it was over.

Neither Stewart nor I had understood unconditional love before all this happened, but this really forced us to learn to love. It's still hard for me because I don't want to let anybody hurt me, and I'm afraid if I love them, they might hurt me. But I'm growing. Melissa's dad genuinely began to love her, hug her, and affirm her, and we began to see a very beautiful person in her with a deep heart and who really cares for people.

Our relationship with her changed so much that she didn't even want to leave us to go off to college. In fact, when she went to college, in the first couple of weeks a guy was interested in taking her out, and she called her dad to ask him what he thought about it. We cried because we were so grateful for the restoration in our relationship. Melissa didn't need to call to ask for permission or advice, but she wanted to talk to her dad about him. It was so different from anything that she would have done before. The Lord has worked so much in all our lives. Today the relationship we have with Melissa is unexplainable apart from the grace of God.

As I think back on all that has happened, I don't see the problem as primarily Melissa's. It is ours, Stewart's and mine—and especially Stewart's. I'm not trying to be hard on him. He did the best he knew how, but he grew up with a father who was emotionally absent. He lacked the skills he needed to be an attentive, loving father to Melissa. Teenage girls need to feel the special, safe love of their fathers. When Stewart began to meet Melissa's emotional needs, then she didn't need Cory to meet them anymore. So I don't see it so much as Melissa's problem as our problem.

Melissa had needs that we didn't see. She looked secure and happy on the outside, but she was lonely and hurting on the inside. A father needs to make his daughter his princess, but before that, he needs to make his wife his queen. If this precious princess can see that her dad loves her mother first and foremost, that gives her security. Then if her dad thinks she is special and that she hung the moon, then the boys she dates are going to have to live up to that standard of what her father was to her. If her father loves her and treats her with dignity and respect, she will look for a husband who treats her the same way—not for what she can do for him, not for what she looks like, or what she accomplished, but for who she is, her heart.

All this with Melissa surfaced problems in our marriage. Melissa thought she had caused the problems, but I had to tell her that she didn't cause them at all. They were already there, but hidden. Stewart and I learned how to argue with each other . . . how to have a good fight and still love each other. Our girls can now see that two people can disagree and still love each other if there is a real commitment to each other. The grass is not greener on the other side! All of this has been very good for Stewart and me—and for our children.

Thank you, Rodney, for letting me tell you our story.

Your friend,

Nancy

I've witnessed courageous men and women choose to change the legacy in their families even if no one else was willing to join them. These faithful people studied, read, prayed, wept, and talked so that the principles of truth and grace became a part of their own lives. Then, and only then, could they impart these qualities to their children.

If you have read through this book, two things are probably true of you: you feel the intense pain of seeing your child in trouble or in conflict, and you desperately want to help your child get back on God's path of purpose and joy. God hasn't promised to change us or our children instantly, but he has promised to be near, even when we feel alone; to forgive us, even when we've failed . . . again; and to give us strength, even when we think we can't go on. The Christian life is a journey, often a difficult journey, of learning and growing—for ourselves and for those we love. God wants to use every circumstance in our lives, including the pain and pleasure of being a parent, to draw us to himself and deepen our faith in him. Ultimately, that's what pleases him—our faithfulness, especially in the most difficult times. And as we trust him to give us grace and strength, God will also work in his own way and in his own timing in the life of the children we cherish. We can be confident of his gracious purposes.

A Closer Look

1. How did you feel as you read Nancy's story about Melissa?

2. What are the main principles from this book that you can implement today and in the coming months?

3. Write your hopeful prayer to God:
   - About yourself as you trust God for wisdom, grace and strength:
   - For your child:
   - For others in your family:

ENDNOTES

Chapter 1

1. Gary Rosberg, *Do-It-Yourself Relationship Mender* (Wheaton, Ill.: Tyndale, 1995), 35–36.

Chapter 2

1. "Cultural Impact," *Group* magazine, Loveland, Colo.: Group Publishing, September–October 1994: 36–38.

Chapter 4

1. Cited in Kaplan and Saccuzzo, *Psychological Testing: Principles, Applications, and Issues* (Belmont, Calif.: Brooks/Cole Publishing Co., 1982), 445–47.
2. Cited by Philip Yancey, *Reaching for the Invisible God* (Grand Rapids, Mich.: Zondervan Publishing House, 2000), 69.

Chapter 5

1. Dan Allender, *The Wounded Heart* (Colorado Springs, Colo.: Navpress, 1990), 158–70.
2. Jeff VanVonderen, *Tired of Trying to Measure Up* (Minneapolis, Mn: Bethany House Publishers, 1989).

Chapter 6

1. Adapted and expanded from Rodney Gage, *The Relationship Revolution* (Nashville, Tenn.: LifeWay Publishing, 1999), 124–25.

Chapter 10

1. David Augsburger, *The Freedom of Forgiveness* (Chicago: Moody Press, 1970), 35–40.
2. Josh McDowell, *How to Be a Hero to Your Kids* (Dallas, London, Vancouver, Melbourne: Word Publishing, 1991), 16.
3. Cited by Josh McDowell, *From Keys to a Revolutionary Involvement on the School Campuses of America*, audiotape.
4. Cited by Zig Ziglar, *Raising Positive Kids in a Negative World*, audiotape.
5. Cited by Jerry Johnston, *How to Save Your Kids from Ruin*, audiotape.

Chapter 11

1. John S. Long and Ronald A. Taylor, "America on Drugs", *U. S. News & World Report* (July 18, 1986), 48–49.
2. Dr. Jean Kilbourne for the National Council of Alcoholism was quoted in *Seventeen* magazine. Cited in Jerry Johnston's book, *It's Killing Our Kids* (Dallas, London, Vancouver, Melbourne: Word Publishing, 1991), introduction, 16.
3. National Council on Alcoholism, Thomas Seessel, Executive director. Cited out of Jerry Johnston's book *Why Suicide* (Nashville: Oliver Nelson, 1987).
4. National Institute on Alcohol Abuse and Alcoholism. Cited out of Jerry Johnston's book *Why Suicide* (Nashville: Oliver Nelson, 1987), 54.
5. Josh McDowell, *Why Wait?* (San Bernardino, CA: Here's Life Publishers, 1987), 40.
6. Josh McDowell, *Right From Wrong* (Dallas, London, Vancouver, Melbourne: Word Publishing, 1994), backcover.
7. Josh McDowell, *How to Be a Hero to Your Kids* (Dallas, London, Vancouver, Melbourne: Word Publishing, 1991), 22.
8. Zig Ziglar, *Raising Positive Kids in a Negative World*, audiotape.
9. Zig Ziglar, *Raising Positive Kids in a Negative World* (New York: Ballentine Books, 1985), 73.
10. The poem "Children Live What They Learn" is often published under "author unknown"; a similar version titled "Children Learn What They Learn" has been published by Dorothy Law Nolte, copyright 1972 and 1975, www.empowermentresources.com/info2/childrenlearn-long_version.html
11. Jerry Johnston, *Who's Listening* (Grand Rapids: Zondervan, 1992), introduction.

ABOUT THE AUTHOR

Rodney Gage is founding pastor of the Fellowship of Orlando located in Orlando, Florida. Gage is also the president of Rodney Gage International, an interdenominational ministry aimed at parents and teenagers alike. Since 1988, Gage has spoken in more than five hundred churches across the country. His "Wise Up" school assembly program has been heard by more than two million students in public and private schools throughout North America, Eastern Europe, Russia, and Brazil.

Gage's *Relationship Revolution* campaign is designed to help parents and youth understand how their key emotional needs have a profound effect on the way they think, feel, and behave. The ultimate impact of this campaign will enhance the emotional and spiritual well-being of parents and teenagers and revolutionize their relationships with family and friends.

Gage is a graduate of Liberty University and Southwestern Baptist Theological Seminary.

Rodney and his wife, Michelle, have three children. They live in Orlando, Florida.

Additional Resources

For further information on scheduling a *Relationship Revolution* event in your church or community, to order resources by Rodney Gage, or to schedule Rodney to speak in your church, school or community, contact:

Rodney Gage International
4231 Inwood Landing Dr.
Orlando, FL 32812
E-mail: rodneygage@aol.com